Sweeten Your Life
the Xylitol Way

Sweeten Your Life
the Xylitol Way

*Delicious recipes
using nature's own
low-calorie sweetener*

Karen Edwards, Ph.D.

Sweeten Your Life the Xylitol Way
by Karen Edwards, Ph.D.

ISBN 0-9746045-0-X

Design by Armour&Armour, Nashville, Tennessee

First Edition 2003
  2 3 4 5 6 7 8 9 10

Acknowledgments

I would like to thank everyone who has given me encouragement, support, and advice in the preparation and publication of this unique cookbook.

Special thanks are due Lorenne Jeré and Dan Bilezikian for encouraging me to create a cookbook using xylitol.

The wonderful folks at the Pensacola Area Center for Enlightened Minds (PACEM) were very helpful with their advice, encouragement, and feedback after sampling many of the completed recipes. I would especially like to thank Ken Chance, Delaine Croonenborgh, Ray Fry, Sharalee Hoelscher, Vickie Knuckles, and Christy Mull. In addition, I wish to express my appreciation to my many other friends and neighbors for their encouragement and support.

The people at Armour&Armour, who were the graphic designers, went out of their way to assist me in many ways that were over and above their normal duties in the preparation of my first published cookbook.

I am very grateful to my husband, Everett, for his patience in dealing with my constant questioning about the recipes' taste, texture, and visual appeal. He was also invaluable in assisting me with editing and proofreading as well as finding some interesting and informative websites.

Contents

Cakes

Pies

Cheesecakes

Cookies

Breads and Muffins

Frostings, Fillings, and Toppings

Drinks, Ice Creams, Etc.

Appendix A

Appendix B

Appendix C

Foreword

The value of xylitol as a sugar substitute was demonstrated in the famous "Turku Sugar Studies" which were conducted in Finland during the early 1970's. Food suppliers were invited to come up with xylitol versions of their standard recipes. After considerable mixing, tweaking, and adjusting, a full line of xylitol replacements emerged. Among these were xylitol pastries, cookies, jams, yogurt, ice cream, candy, soft drinks, pickles, relish, mustard, and ketchup. One group of young adult volunteers was given these specially prepared foods in which xylitol replaced sugar wherever possible. Most of them considered their xylitol diet comparable or superior to a regular sugar diet. The most outstanding finding from Turku was that a xylitol diet practically eliminated the development of tooth decay. The results were so encouraging that a parallel study was begun to test xylitol in chewing gum. Used this way, xylitol produced similar dental benefits at a much lower consumption level.

For the next 20 years, research focused on using small amounts of xylitol in delivery systems targeted to protect teeth. During this time, xylitol was considered too scarce and expensive to be practical as a general purpose sugar substitute. In some countries such as Germany and Russia, xylitol continued to be used as a premium sweetener in the diabetic diet. More recently there has been a trend for an increased supply and decreased price for xylitol. This has prompted more interest in xylitol for applications beyond chewing gum and toothpaste. Consumers found that xylitol has many qualities that make it suitable for their dietary goals: good functional sweetness with reduced calories and very low Glycemic Index (reduced impact on blood sugar and insulin). There is also evidence for some prebiotic and satiety effects. Some of these beneficial properties result from the slow absorption and metabolism of xylitol. As with dietary fiber (think beans!), too much xylitol at one time can lead to intestinal gas and loose stools. Most people adapt quickly to tolerate increasing amounts of xylitol. Begin by using a small amount of xylitol, such as gum or mints, after each meal. Allow yourself two weeks to gradually build up your comfort level.

It is interesting to look back at the Turku studies and realize that the sugar consumption level was only about half of what much of the population consumes today. Even with a healthy sweet such as xylitol, moderation is the sensible approach. Have fun with the recipes, and enjoy a little sweetness. The smiles are worth it.

John Peldyak, D.M.D.
July 2003

Introduction

There must be literally thousands of cookbooks of all kinds, sizes, and types of cuisine on the market today. I have seen everything from vegan cookbooks to recipes using Coca-Cola. Why, in the world then, would I want to compile another cookbook with so much competition out there? The idea started with a vague feeling that somehow there was a relationship between the food I was eating and my overall health. Over a period of several years I became more aware of my body and that I had developed a host of chronic medical concerns. At first I blamed the majority of these on heredity, noting that many of my relatives had experienced similar health problems over the years and had developed even more serious conditions such as cancer and heart disease. I knew that I did not want my health to deteriorate to the point where I might also develop these diseases. Because I had begun to have less and less success in improving my health using conventional medical techniques and treatments, I began an intensive search into more natural healing methods.

As my awareness of alternative healing methods increased, I realized that I wanted a more formal education in this field than I could get through simply reading magazine articles, talking to others about their anecdotal experiences, and gleaning information from an herbal company that I had become associated with. I decided to enroll in Clayton College of Natural Health in Birmingham, Alabama, because they offered a program and degrees in holistic nutrition, and I could complete the course of study at home. I had always enjoyed cooking and preparing meals that were not only healthy but were also satisfying to the taste, and I thought that combining this interest with a more thorough knowledge of nutrition would benefit not only me, but my husband as well.

As I progressed through my studies, I learned more and more details about the effects that different foods have on the body and which foods were most beneficial to our health. Foods that have undergone the least amount of refining contain more nutrients than highly refined foods, and consequently, are better able to help restore optimal health within the body. On the other hand, highly refined and processed foods, while appealing to the sensory pleasures of taste, smell, and texture, are in most cases devoid of the nutrients necessary for the body to maintain optimal health.

For several years I had been compiling a number of traditional recipes that I had modified using healthier ingredients. For instance, I used honey, molasses, and organic sugar as sweeteners, but even though these natural sweeteners were more nutritious than refined sugar, research into nutrition for my doctorate showed that they not only fed the bacteria that caused tooth decay, they also contributed to other situations (i.e., elevated blood sugar levels, ear, bladder and yeast infections). I began to search for other alternative sweeteners to replace these in my recipes, and found two products that met my requirements: stevia and xylitol. Stevia, while much sweeter than sugar, could only be used in small quantities, and did not give adequate results in making desserts because of its lack of bulk. However, I learned that granulated xylitol could be substituted directly for sugar, and I decided to try it in recipes that I made for my family and friends. The results were so outstanding that I was able to modify almost all of my recipes so that xylitol was the only sweetener used. I discovered two exceptions to the general rule that xylitol can be substituted directly for sugar. These are that xylitol does not caramelize or brown similar to refined sugar, and it also will not feed yeast, which prevents it from being used in recipes where dough needs to rise. However, xylitol can be used in most other types of baked goods and desserts.

People began to ask for my recipes, but they had never heard of xylitol and were unaware that it occurs naturally in fruits and vegetables. Some of my acquaintances were fearful that it was an artificial sweetener such as aspartame or saccharin. I had already planned to publish a cookbook for people who were wishing to make the transition from traditional recipes to a healthier cooking style. This cookbook contained all types and kinds of recipes for a wide variety of foods including desserts. I mentioned this cookbook to the lady from the company I usually ordered xylitol from, and she was so interested that she insisted that I talk to the product manager of the company. He was very interested also and encouraged me to write a cookbook with recipes using xylitol exclusively as the sweetener because there were no cookbooks on the market like this.

Based on the overwhelmingly positive response to the modified recipes from my family and friends and because of the encouragement of the product manager, I decided to write this cookbook. My goal is to help others become more aware of the benefits of using xylitol, and to see how easy it is to use. I have proven that recipes made with whole foods and more nutritious ingredients can taste delicious and have an appealing texture. Even though most of us desire an occassional dessert, we can now enjoy a treat without all of the guilt and realize that healthy desserts can truly taste good. In order to increase the nutritional value of these recipes, I have also eliminated refined flours, and reduced the fat content of many of the recipes by 50 percent or more.

I hope you get as much enjoyment and benefits from making these recipes as I have, and I encourage you to experiment further with your own recipes to make them healthier using xylitol along with more natural ingredients.

About Xylitol

What is xylitol, where does it come from, and why is it important? These and other facts about this unique sweetener will be answered here for your information and enlightenment. Xylitol is a five-carbon sugar alcohol, or polyol, (chemical formula: $C_5H_{12}O_5$; molecular weight: 152.15) that can be synthesized from a number of natural products, but primarily from the bark of birch trees. Even though it is synthesized, it is considered a natural substance because its chemical composition is identical to the naturally occurring substance. It is an odorless white crystalline powder with the same sweetness and bulk as sucrose (sugar), but having 40% less calories. It is metabolized in the body as a normal carbohydrate, but at a much slower rate than refined sugar (sucrose). It has no aftertaste and exhibits a very pleasant cooling sensation when it dissolves in the mouth. It occurs naturally in many fruits and vegetables and is even made in the human body during its normal metabolism of glucose at the rate of about 10 to 15 grams daily.

Historically xylitol was discovered in 1891 by Emil Fischer, a German chemist. It was used chiefly as a research chemical until World War II resulted in a shortage of sugar in some European countries such as Finland. Finnish researchers and engineers succeeded in developing an industrial method for xylitol production on a small scale to provide an alternative sweetener. However, the end of the war removed the sugar shortage, and xylitol production was not pursued again until 1975 when the Finns began large-scale production. A Swiss company, F. Hoffman La-Roche, joined with the Finnish Sugar Co. in 1976 to found Xyrofin that later became a wholly owned subsidiary of the Finnish Sugar Co. (currently Cultor). Prior to 1970, companies located in the Soviet Union, China, Japan, Germany, Italy, and others produced xylitol mainly for domestic use as a sweetener in diabetic diets and in IV infusion therapy to alleviate insulin shock and coma. The first xylitol chewing gum was produced and distributed both in Finland and the USA in 1975. Today, xylitol is not only available in bulk form, but is also found in many products such as mints, toothpastes, mouthwashes, confections, pharmaceuticals, and dietetic and diabetic foods.

Because of xylitol's 5-carbon structure, many types of bacteria such as *Streptococcus* cannot metabolize it, whereas the 6-carbon sugars such as sucrose do support bacterial growth. This is the key reason that xylitol has been found to be effective in preventing or reducing cavities and sinus infections and inhibiting the growth of bacteria that cause ear infections in children. It may even prevent lung infections, according to recent research into therapies for cystic fibrosis. Many research studies conducted over more than 30 years have confirmed that using xylitol in the form of chewing gum from 3 to 5 times a day (about 4 to 12 grams per day) will reduce or prevent dental caries. In the United States, xylitol is approved as a food additive in unlimited quantities for foods with special dietary purposes. Xylitol is useful as a sweetener in foods for persons who have diabetes because of its low glycemic index of 7 (sugar is rated at 100) and its reduced caloric value (2.4

calories per gram vs. 4.0 for sugar). This was the first medical use of xylitol. Insulin is required to get glucose into the cells, which is a problem for diabetics. Because xylitol is metabolized into glycogen that can be stored directly in the cells until it is converted into glucose for energy, no insulin is therefore required. Also, because xylitol is slowly absorbed and is a natural insulin stabilizer, the rapid rise in blood glucose levels normally associated with the ingestion of sugar is greatly reduced. Other benefits of xylitol include prevention of *Candida Albicans*, because it inhibits yeast growth, and it increases the absorption of B vitamins and calcium, thus aiding in bone remineralization, which may help to prevent the onset of osteoporosis.

Xylitol is considered safe for human consumption and is an approved food additive. The Federation of American Societies for Experimental Biology confirmed this in a study in 1986 prepared at the request of the U.S. Food and Drug Administration. The Joint Expert Committee on Food Additives not only verified that xylitol was safe for humans, but also discounted adverse findings in a 1970 animal study by stating that a review of the results were found not to be relevant to humans. This committee, which is an advisory body to the World Health Organization and the United Nations, allocated an Acceptable Daily Intake of "not specified" which is the safest category that a food additive can be given. In addition, the European Union has accepted xylitol as acceptable for dietary use.

There are few disadvantages to xylitol. It is more expensive than sugar and is not easily found in grocery or health food stores. However, this disadvantage may become less relevant in the future as there are a number of research programs now underway to make xylitol from less costly raw materials and to reduce the cost by utilizing new and more efficient production methods. Also, as the popularity of using xylitol increases and the resulting sales volume increases, the cost will certainly decrease in the future. If xylitol has never been used before, ingesting a large amount at one time can result in a loose stool, but this problem disappears quickly because adaptation to xylitol is very rapid. Regular use reduces this small side effect, and most people can accept about 100 grams daily if individual servings are limited to 20 – 30 grams each.

For more information concerning xylitol, the following references are listed for your convenience:

- "Xylitol, Sweeten Your Smile," a booklet by John Peldyak, DMD, 1996, now out of print but can be found on the Internet through used bookstores or downloaded from www.xylitol.org.
- www.xylitol.info
- www.caloriecontrol.org/xylitol.html
- www.principalhealthnews.com
- www.tifac.org.in/news/view6.htm
- www.pharmj.com/Editorial/20001014/clinical/xylitol_543.html

Helpful Hints

In today's hectic, fast-paced world, it appears that an increasing number of people are searching for quick and easy recipes with a minimum number of ingredients. In compiling these recipes, I have focused on using whole foods and the freshest ingredients. I have found that employing this combination of top-quality ingredients produces delicious results that are far more satisfying than those recipes that are made from mixes found in grocery stores and foods prepared by even the best restaurants. These hints are offered to help you obtain optimal flavor and health benefits from the recipes in this cookbook.

SELECTING FRUIT. When preparing a recipe requiring fruit, select fruit at its peak of ripeness, because fruit that has ripened has a fuller, richer, and sweeter flavor than fruit that has not fully ripened or is overripe. Also it should be noted that overripe or under ripe fruit, or fruit that has had a long storage period, loses essential nutrients such as vitamins and enzymes.

ORGANIC INGREDIENTS. Buy and use organic ingredients whenever possible. This is becoming more important every day in order to avoid toxins such as herbicides, pesticides, by products of the petrochemical industries, emulsifiers, antibiotics, and growth hormones. In addition, organic produce is grown with natural fertilizers that contain all of the necessary minerals needed to grow healthy plants, whereas artificial fertilizers contain only a small portion of these vital minerals. Organic fruits should be washed under running water and scrubbed with a vegetable brush before using. If organic fruits are not used, be sure to scrub them with a vegetable brush after spraying with a produce cleanser and then rinse or soak thoroughly.

PIE SHELLS. Pre-baking a pie shell is my preference in order to avoid a soggy crust. To pre-bake the bottom crust, fit the pastry into the pie plate, and refrigerate for at least 30 minutes before baking to keep the decorative edging intact when it is placed into the pre-heated oven. Remove from the refrigerator, line the pastry with parchment paper covering the edge of the crust, and fill with any type of dried beans, which can be reused many times. Bake at 425° for 15 minutes, and remove the pie shell from the oven. Remove the beans and parchment paper. Using a fork, prick completely through the pastry all over the bottom and sides to prevent bubbles from forming. If a filling containing a large amount of liquid such as a custard-type filling is to be added, then prick only halfway through the pastry with the fork. Return the pie shell to the oven, and bake for an additional 5 minutes prior to adding uncooked fillings. Bake 5 more minutes or until completely done for cooked fillings.

PAN SIZE. The size of the pans used in baking cakes is critical. If the pan used is smaller than required, the batter may rise excessively and spill over the edge of the pan, or the cake may sink in the middle as it cools. Another result of using too small a pan is a coarse-textured cake. If the pan used is larger than required, the cake will look flat because it will not be able to rise sufficiently. Make sure that baking pans are one-half to two-thirds full of batter.

ICE CREAM. The ice cream made from these recipes does not tend to form ice crystals when stored in the freezer. However, if you experience problems with ice crystals, wrap the container in heavy aluminum foil each time it is returned to the freezer.

SELECTING BAKING CHOCOLATE. I have found it to be very important to use a high quality unsweetened chocolate in these recipes. Some of the unsweetened bar chocolate on the market today seems to have a bitter or overly strong taste, even when combined with other ingredients. In developing these recipes, I used Ghiradelli unsweetened baking chocolate.

USING MELTED CHOCOLATE. An easy way to drizzle chocolate over cakes or cookies is to first melt the chocolate in a microwave oven or a double boiler on the range top. Spoon the melted chocolate into a corner of a small, plastic resealable bag, and cut off a tiny edge of the corner. Now it is ready to use like a pastry bag.

POWDERED XYLITOL. Powdered xylitol is commercially available and can be substituted for powdered sugar on a one-to-one basis.

WATER BATH. A water bath ensures more even baking than the normal dry heat of an oven, and it is an excellent method for preventing or greatly reducing the risk of cracking the top surface of a cheesecake. This method also results in a cheesecake with a moist and creamy texture and eliminates the need for adding flour or another starch to the recipe. Place the cheesecake in a springform pan on a large sheet of heavy-duty aluminum foil, bringing the edges of the foil up the sides to the top of the pan. This will prevent any water from seeping into the cheesecake while it is baking. Place the springform pan in the center of a large roasting pan and pour in hot water to a depth of 1½". Then bake as directed by the recipe.

Kitchen Measures And Substitutions

Liquid Measurements

¼ cup = 2 fluid ounces
½ cup = 4 fluid ounces
1 cup = 8 fluid ounces
2 cups = 16 fluid ounces
4 cups = 32 fluid ounces
2 cups = 1 pint
2 pints = 1 quart
4 cups = 1 quart

Dry Measurements

3 teaspoons = 1 tablespoon
2 tablespoons = ⅛ cup
4 tablespoons = ¼ cup
5⅓ tablespoons = ⅓ cup
8 tablespoons = ½ cup
16 tablespoons = 1 cup

Be sure to measure accurately. Measure dry ingredients by lightly spooning ingredient into dry measuring cup. Use flat edge of knife to level off the top after each measure. Use measuring spoons for quantities less than ¼ cup. Dip measuring spoon into ingredient to be measured, and use knife to level off the top.

Measure liquid ingredients in a glass measuring cup. Place the cup on a solid surface at eye level. Fill cup to desired mark.

Substitutions

2 tablespoons flour for thickening = 1 tablespoon arrowroot powder

1 teaspoon baking powder = ¼ teaspoon baking soda
+½ teaspoon cream of tartar

1 cup sour cream = 1 cup plain whole milk yogurt

1 ounce unsweetened baking chocolate = 3 tablespoons unsweetened
cocoa powder
+ 1 tablespoon unsalted butter

4 ounces semi-sweet chocolate bar = 2 ounces unsweetened
chocolate bar
+ ⅓ cup xylitol

6 ounces (1 cup) semi-sweet chocolate chips, melted = 6 tablespoons unsweetened
cocoa powder
+ 7 tablespoons xylitol
+ 4 tablespoons unsalted butter

4 ounce bar of sweet cooking chocolate = 4 tablespoons unsweetened
cocoa powder
+ 5 tablespoons xylitol
+ 3 tablespoons unsalted butter

Cakes

Applesauce Spice Cake

4 tablespoons unsalted butter
⅔ cup xylitol
1½ cups plus 2 tablespoons unsweetened applesauce
2 eggs
2 cups spelt flour or whole wheat pastry flour
1½ teaspoons baking powder
½ teaspoon baking soda
⅛ teaspoon salt
1½ teaspoon cinnamon
¼ teaspoon cloves
½ teaspoon nutmeg
½ teaspoon allspice
1 cup finely chopped apples
½ cup raisins (optional)

Rehydrate raisins by covering them with warm water and allowing to soak for at least 30 minutes. Cream butter and xylitol; gradually add 2 tablespoons applesauce during creaming process. Beat in eggs. Stir in remaining 1½ cups applesauce. Combine flour, baking powder, baking soda, salt, and spices. Slowly add dry ingredients into creamed mixture, stirring well after each addition. Stir in chopped apples and drained raisins. Pour batter into buttered and floured 8" square baking pan. Bake at 350° for 40-45 minutes or until toothpick inserted in center comes out clean. **Yield: 16 servings**

Per Serving: **Fat:** 3.9g **Carbs:** 24.6g **Fiber:** 2.6g **Cal:** 135

Banana Cake

¾ cup oat flour
1 cup spelt flour or whole wheat pastry flour
⅜ teaspoon salt
½ teaspoon baking soda
⅔ cup xylitol
2 eggs
1 cup pureed ripe bananas
4 tablespoons extra-virgin olive oil
¼ cup unsweetened applesauce (or pureed bananas)
1 teaspoon vanilla extract

In a large bowl, combine flours, salt, baking soda, and xylitol. In another bowl, mix together eggs, pureed bananas, oil, applesauce, and vanilla extract. Add liquid ingredients all at once to the flour mixture, and stir just until dry ingredients are moistened. Pour batter into buttered 8" square baking pan and bake at 350° for 25-30 minutes or until toothpick inserted in center comes out clean. **Yield: 16 servings**

Note: This cake is delicious served just as it is, or it may be topped off with Lemon Cream Cheese Frosting, page 62.

Per Serving: Fat: 4.9g **Carbs:** 21g **Fiber:** 1.7g **Cal:** 126

Black Forest Cake

Cake:
> 5 eggs
> ⅔ cup xylitol
> 1 teaspoon vanilla extract
> ½ cup spelt flour or whole wheat pastry flour
> ¼ cup unsweetened cocoa powder
> ¼ cup arrowroot powder
> Cherry Syrup, see below
> Whipped Cream Frosting, page 64
> Cherry Topping, page 60

Cherry Syrup:
> ½ cup water
> ½ cup xylitol
> 2 tablespoons cherry liqueur

To prepare cake: Beat eggs and xylitol with an electric mixer for 5-10 minutes, or until pale and creamy. Stir in vanilla extract. Combine flour, cocoa powder, and arrowroot powder; sift over egg mixture, and gently fold in. Cut a piece of parchment paper to fit the bottom of two 8" round cake pans. (Do not grease the pans and do not use non-stick pans.) Pour batter into the pans. Bake at 350° for 18-22 minutes or until toothpick inserted in center comes out clean. To prevent cake from shrinking, do not remove from pan while it is still warm. After removing cake from oven, turn cake upside down and rest edges of pan on other pans until cake has completely cooled.

To prepare cherry syrup: Place water and xylitol in a small saucepan and bring to a boil, stirring until xylitol is completely dissolved. Allow mixture to come to a low boil, and continue boiling for 5 minutes without stirring. Cool syrup before adding cherry liqueur. Prick top of each cake layer with a fork 15-20 times. Spoon half of cherry syrup over each cake layer.

To assemble Black Forest Cake: Place one layer on serving plate, top with half of the Whipped Cream Frosting, and add the second layer. Spoon Cherry Topping onto second layer. Frost sides of cake with remaining Whipped Cream Frosting. Refrigerate until serving. **Yield: 16 servings**

Per Serving: Fat: 7.4g **Carbs:** 30g **Fiber:** 1.1g **Cal:** 177

Blueberry Snack Cake

Cake:
- 1 cup spelt flour or whole wheat pastry flour
- ⅓ cup xylitol
- 2 teaspoon baking powder
- ½ teaspoon salt
- 1 egg
- ⅓ cup plain low-fat yogurt
- 3 tablespoons water
- 1½ tablespoons extra-virgin olive oil
- 4 tablespoons unsweetened applesauce
- 1 tablespoon fresh lemon juice
- 1 cup blueberries

Topping:
- ⅓ cup xylitol
- ¼ cup spelt flour or whole wheat pastry flour
- ¼ teaspoon cinnamon
- ⅓ cup finely ground almonds
- 1 tablespoon unsalted butter

To prepare cake batter: In a medium bowl, combine flour, xylitol, baking powder, and salt. In another bowl, mix together egg, yogurt, water, oil, applesauce, and lemon juice. Add liquid ingredients all at once to flour mixture, and stir just until dry ingredients are moistened. Pour batter into a buttered 8" square pan; sprinkle with blueberries.

To prepare topping: Combine xylitol, flour, cinnamon, and almonds. Cut in butter until mixture is crumbly; sprinkle topping over blueberries. Bake at 325° for 35-40 minutes or until toothpick inserted in center comes out clean. Cover with foil, if needed, during last part of baking to avoid over-browning. **Yield: 16 servings**

Per Serving: Fat: 4g **Carbs:** 18.2g **Fiber:** 1.9g **Cal:** 107

Butterscotch Pecan Cake Squares

1½ tablespoons unsalted butter, melted
1½ tablespoons extra-virgin olive oil
3 tablespoons unsweetened applesauce
¾ cup xylitol
2 eggs, lightly beaten
2 teaspoons vanilla extract
1 cup spelt flour or whole wheat pastry flour
1½ teaspoon baking powder
½ teaspoon salt
⅓ cup chopped pecans

In medium bowl, combine melted butter, oil, applesauce, and xylitol. Add the eggs and vanilla extract and mix well. In a small bowl, combine flour, baking powder, salt, and pecans. Gradually add liquid ingredients into flour mixture, and stir to mix well. Pour batter into buttered 8" square pan. Bake at 350° for 15-20 minutes or until toothpick inserted in center comes out clean. **Yield: 16 servings**

Note: These have a cake-like texture with a delicate butterscotch-pecan flavor.

Per Serving: Fat: 4.9g **Carbs:** 16g **Fiber:** 1.2g **Cal:** 103

Carrot Cake

2 cups spelt flour or whole wheat pastry flour
1½ teaspoons lecithin granules
2 teaspoons baking powder
1 teaspoon baking soda
½ teaspoon salt
½ teaspoon ginger
2 teaspoons cinnamon
¼ teaspoon nutmeg
1 cup xylitol
2 teaspoons vanilla extract
½ cup plain low-fat yogurt
¼ cup extra-virgin olive oil
3 eggs, separated
2 cups grated carrots
1 small can crushed pineapple (in its own juice)
⅓ cup shredded unsweetened coconut

Combine flour, lecithin, baking powder, baking soda, salt, spices, and xylitol in a large bowl. In a medium bowl, mix vanilla extract, yogurt, oil, and egg yolks. Add liquid ingredients and briefly beat. Stir in carrots, pineapple (with juice), and coconut. Beat egg whites till stiff but not dry; gently but thoroughly fold beaten egg whites into cake batter. Pour batter into 2 buttered and floured 9" cake pans and bake at 375° for 20-25 minutes or until toothpick inserted in center comes out clean. **Yield: 20 servings**

Note: The traditional frosting for this cake is Lemon Cream Cheese Frosting, page 62.

Per Serving: Fat: 11.5g **Carbs:** 29.4g **Fiber:** 2.2g **Cal:** 216

Chocolate Cake Squares

2 cups spelt flour or whole wheat pastry flour
1¾ cups xylitol
2 teaspoons baking soda
4 tablespoons unsalted butter
1 cup minus 2 tablespoons water
¼ cup unsweetened cocoa powder
6 tablespoons prune puree
½ cup plain low-fat yogurt
2 large eggs
1 teaspoon vanilla extract
1 (1.5 oz.) maltitol-sweetened dark chocolate bar (optional)

In a large bowl, combine flour, xylitol, and baking soda. In a saucepan, combine butter, water, and cocoa powder; bring to a boil, then remove from heat. Stir in prune puree. Pour this mixture over dry ingredients, and stir until blended. Stir in yogurt, eggs, and vanilla extract. Pour batter into buttered and floured 9" x 13" pan. Bake at 350° for 20-25 minutes or until toothpick inserted in center comes out clean. Allow cake to thoroughly cool, then spread with frosting. Crème de Menthe Cream Cheese Frosting, page 62, or Mocha Cream Cheese Frosting, page 63, are excellent toppings for this cake. Cut into squares and serve. If desired, melt chocolate bar and drizzle chocolate onto frosted cake squares. **Yield: 24 servings**

Per Serving: **Fat:** 2.7g **Carbs:** 23.6g **Fiber:** 1.6g **Cal:** 109

Chocolate Pound Cake

½ cup unsalted butter, softened
2½ cups xylitol
⅓ cup reduced-fat sour cream
½ cup plus 3 tablespoons plain low-fat yogurt
5 eggs
3 cups spelt flour or whole wheat pastry flour
2½ teaspoons baking powder
½ teaspoon salt
1 tablespoon lecithin granules
3 tablespoons unsweetened cocoa powder
2 teaspoons vanilla extract

Cream butter and xylitol until light and fluffy, about 5 minutes. Gradually beat in sour cream and 3 tablespoons of yogurt to butter mixture during creaming process. Add eggs, one at a time, beating just until blended.

Combine flour, baking powder, salt, lecithin, and cocoa powder. With mixer on low speed, add dry ingredients, alternately with remaining ½ cup yogurt, to creamed mixture, beginning and ending with flour. Stir in vanilla extract. Pour batter into a buttered and floured 10" tube pan; bake at 325° for 1 hour or until toothpick inserted in center comes out clean. Cool cake in pan for 10 minutes, then remove from pan and cool completely before serving. **Yield: 20 servings**

Per Serving: **Fat:** 6.9g **Carbs:** 40.4g **Fiber:** 2.6g **Cal:** 210

German Chocolate Cake

Chocolate Mixture:
>   3 tablespoons unsweetened cocoa powder
>   ⅓ cup xylitol
>   1 tablespoon plus 2 teaspoons unsalted butter
>   2 teaspoons prune puree (or unsweetened applesauce)
>   ½ cup hot water

Cake:
>   ½ cup unsalted butter
>   2 cups (minus 1 tablespoon) xylitol
>   4 tablespoons prune puree (or unsweetened applesauce)
>   4 eggs, separated
>   1 teaspoon vanilla extract
>   2¼ cups spelt flour or whole wheat pastry flour
>   1 teaspoon baking soda
>   ¼ teaspoon salt
>   ¾ cup plain low-fat yogurt combined with ¼ cup water

To prepare chocolate mixture: In a saucepan, combine above ingredients. Cook over low heat, stirring constantly, until mixture is smooth. Turn off heat, and set aside.

To prepare cake batter: In a large mixing bowl, cream butter and xylitol; gradually add prune puree during creaming process. Beat in egg yolks, one at a time, just until blended. Add cooled chocolate mixture and vanilla extract, and stir to mix well.

Combine flour, baking soda, and salt; add to the creamed mixture alternately with yogurt and water, beginning and ending with flour mixture. Beat egg whites until stiff but not dry, and gently fold into batter.

Pour cake batter into buttered and floured 9" x 13" pan, and bake at 350° for 35-40 minutes or until toothpick inserted in center comes out clean. Allow cake to cool 10 minutes before removing from pan. If glass baking pan is used, cake may be frosted and served from the pan. **Yield: 24 servings**

Note: The traditional frosting for this cake is Coconut-Pecan Frosting, page 61.

Per Serving without Frosting:
Fat: 5.8g **Carbs:** 28.5g **Fiber:** 1.7g **Cal:** 154

Heavenly Spice Cake

Cake:

    4 tablespoons unsalted butter

    ¾ cup xylitol

    2 tablespoons prune puree

    2 eggs

    2 cups spelt flour or whole wheat pastry flour

    ½ teaspoon cinnamon

    ½ teaspoon allspice

    1 teaspoon baking soda

    ½ cup plain low-fat yogurt

    ⅔ cup prunes, diced and cooked

Frosting:

    ½ cup reduced-fat sour cream

    2 tablespoons unsalted butter

    1 egg, slightly beaten

    ⅔ cup xylitol

    ½ cup prunes, diced and cooked

    ½ cup chopped pecans (optional)

To prepare cake batter: Cream butter and xylitol; gradually add prune puree during creaming process. Add eggs and beat until light and fluffy. Combine flour, cinnamon, and allspice; gradually add to creamed mixture. Combine yogurt and baking soda; add to batter and mix well. Stir in cooked prunes. Spoon batter into a buttered 9" x 13" pan, and bake at 350° for 15-20 minutes or until toothpick inserted in center comes out clean.

To prepare frosting: In a saucepan, combine sour cream, butter, egg, and xylitol. Cook over medium low heat, stirring constantly, until slightly thickened. Stir in pecans and prunes. Spread topping over cooled cake. Refrigerate until ready to serve. **Yield: 24 servings**

Per Serving with Frosting:
Fat: 5.6g   **Carbs:** 33.6g   **Fiber:** 2.2g   **Cal:** 172

Kahlua Cake

1 cup pitted dates, finely chopped
1 tablespoon instant coffee powder
1 cup boiling water
½ cup Kahlua (coffee liqueur)
4 tablespoons unsalted butter, softened
1¼ cups xylitol
½ cup unsweetened applesauce
3 eggs
½ teaspoon vanilla extract
2¾ cups spelt flour or whole wheat pastry flour
1½ teaspoons lecithin granules
1½ teaspoons baking soda
½ teaspoon salt
¼ teaspoon cinnamon

In a medium bowl, combine dates, coffee powder, and boiling water. Stir until coffee powder is completely dissolved; add Kahlua and set aside.

In a large bowl, cream butter and xylitol; gradually add applesauce during creaming process. Beat in eggs, one at a time. Stir in vanilla extract. In another bowl, combine flour, lecithin, baking soda, salt, and cinnamon. Stir flour mixture into creamed ingredients alternately with date mixture, beginning and ending with flour.

Pour into a buttered and floured 9" x 13" pan, and bake at 350° for 25-30 minutes or until toothpick inserted in center comes out clean. Allow cake to cool 10 minutes before removing from pan. **Yield: 24 servings**

Per Serving: Fat: 3g **Carbs:** 30.3g **Fiber:** 2.3g **Cal:** 154

Overnight Coffee Cake

Cake:
- 4 tablespoons unsalted butter
- ¾ cup xylitol
- 4 tablespoons unsweetened applesauce
- 2 eggs
- 1 cup plain low-fat yogurt
- 2 cups spelt flour or whole wheat pastry flour
- 1½ tablespoons lecithin granules
- 1 teaspoon baking powder
- 1 teaspoon baking soda
- ½ teaspoon salt
- 1 teaspoon nutmeg

Topping:
- ⅔ cup xylitol
- ½ cup finely chopped pecans
- 1 teaspoon cinnamon

To prepare cake batter: Cream butter and xylitol; gradually add applesauce during creaming process. Beat in eggs. Add yogurt and mix well. Combine flour, lecithin, baking powder, baking soda, salt, and nutmeg; gradually add to cake batter and mix well. Pour batter into a buttered and floured 9" x 13" x 2" pan.

To prepare topping: Combine xylitol, pecans, and cinnamon. Sprinkle evenly over batter. Cover cake and refrigerate at least 8 hours or overnight. Uncover and bake at 350° for 25-30 minutes or until toothpick inserted in center comes out clean. **Yield: 24 servings**

Note: This sweet, delicately-flavored coffee cake has a very light and tender texture.

Per Serving: Fat: 4.7g **Carbs:** 21g **Fiber:** 1.5g **Cal:** 119

Pineapple Upside-Down Cake

Topping:
>2 tablespoons unsalted butter
>⅓ cup xylitol
>1 small can sliced pineapple (in its own juice), reserve juice
>   to use in topping and cake
>10-12 fresh cherries, halved with pits removed

Cake:
>2½ tablespoons unsalted butter
>½ cup xylitol
>2½ tablespoons unsweetened applesauce
>2 eggs
>2 cups spelt flour or whole wheat pastry flour
>1 tablespoon lecithin granules
>1 teaspoon baking soda
>½ cup plain low-fat yogurt
>1 teaspoon vanilla extract

To prepare topping: In a 9" square baking pan, melt butter. Stir 2 tablespoons of pineapple juice, and ⅓ cup xylitol into melted butter. Arrange pineapple slices over bottom of pan, and place cherry halves (rounded side down) in center of each pineapple slice and between pineapple slices. Set pan aside while preparing cake.

To prepare cake batter: Cream butter and ½ cup xylitol; gradually add applesauce during creaming process, then beat in eggs. In a separate bowl, combine flour, lecithin, and baking soda. In a small bowl, combine yogurt, ¼ cup pineapple juice, and vanilla extract. Gradually add flour, alternately with yogurt mixture, to creamed ingredients. Gently spoon batter into pan. Bake at 350° for 20-25 minutes or until toothpick inserted in center comes out clean. Remove from oven, place serving plate over cake, and immediately invert cake onto plate. This cake is best when served warm. **Yield: 16 servings**

Note: This cake may also be baked in a 10" round cast iron skillet.

Per Serving: **Fat:** 4.6g **Carbs:** 26g **Fiber:** 2.3g **Cal:** 146

Spongecake

5 eggs, separated
1 cup xylitol, divided
1½ teaspoons grated lemon zest
1½ tablespoons fresh lemon juice
2 tablespoons water
¾ cup plus 2 tablespoons spelt flour or whole wheat pastry flour
½ teaspoon salt
½ teaspoon cream of tartar

Using an electric mixer at high speed, beat egg yolks until well blended. Gradually beat ½ cup xylitol into egg yolks. Combine lemon zest, lemon juice, and water. Gradually add the lemon mixture to egg yolks, and beat until light and fluffy. Gently fold flour into egg yolk mixture until all ingredients are well blended.

In a separate bowl, beat egg whites and salt until foamy. Add cream of tartar, and continue beating until soft peaks form. Gradually beat remaining ½ cup xylitol into egg whites. Gently fold egg yolk mixture into beaten egg whites until no streaks of yellow or white are visible.

Cut a piece of parchment paper to fit the bottom of two 9" round cake pans. (Do not grease the pans and do not use non-stick pans.) Spoon batter into the pans. Bake at 350° for 20-25 minutes or until toothpick inserted in center comes out clean. To prevent cake from shrinking, do not remove it from the pan while it is warm. After removing cake from oven, turn cake upside down and support edges of pan on other pans or on some other type of support to prevent top surface of cake from touching anything else, and allow to remain in this position until cake has completely cooled. **Yield: 2 (9") layer cakes (each layer = 8 servings)**

Note: This cake is perfect as a base for Strawberry or Peach Shortcake. Onto one layer of cake, spoon strawberries or peaches (that have been sweetened with xylitol), and top with sweetened whipped cream. If desired, a second layer of cake may be used, with additional strawberries or peaches, and another layer of whipped cream.

Per Serving: Fat: 1.8g **Carbs:** 17.8g **Fiber:** 0.9g **Cal:** 82

Pies

Apple Crisp

6 cups thinly sliced apples
1 cup quick-cooking oats
¼ cup spelt flour or whole wheat pastry flour
½ teaspoon cinnamon
½ cup xylitol
¼ teaspoon maple flavoring
6 tablespoons unsalted butter
¼ cup chopped pecans

Place apple slices in a buttered 9" square baking pan. Combine oats, flour, cinnamon, xylitol, and maple flavoring. Cut in butter until mixture is crumbly, and spoon over apples. Bake at 350° for 40-45 minutes or until apples can be easily pierced with a knife and topping is golden brown. Do not allow topping to darken as this will result in a bitter taste.
Yield: 12 servings

Per Serving: Fat: 8g **Carbs:** 24.5g **Fiber:** 3.3g **Cal:** 150

Apple Pie With Streusel Topping

Apple Filling:
8 cups thinly sliced, cored apples
1 tablespoon freshly squeezed lemon juice
½ cup xylitol
1 tablespoon arrowroot powder *
⅛ teaspoon salt
½ teaspoon grated lemon zest
¼ teaspoon nutmeg
1 teaspoon cinnamon
1 tablespoon unsalted butter
10" pie shell, page 26

Streusel Topping:
⅓ cup xylitol
⅔ cup spelt flour or whole wheat pastry flour
½ cup chopped pecans
1 teaspoon cinnamon
1 teaspoon vanilla extract
¼ teaspoon maple flavoring
4½ tablespoons unsalted butter

To make apple filling: Place apple slices in large bowl, and stir in lemon juice. Mix xylitol, arrowroot powder, salt, lemon zest, nutmeg, and cinnamon; sprinkle over apples. Stir well to evenly distribute cinnamon mixture. Place sweetened apple mixture in pie shell; dot with butter.

To make streusel topping: Combine xylitol, flour, pecans, and cinnamon. Stir in vanilla extract and maple flavoring. Cut in butter until crumbly. Sprinkle topping over apples.

Make a tent with foil and cover pie, cut several slits in foil for steam to escape, and bake at 425° for 1 hour. Reduce oven temperature to 400°, remove foil, and bake another 20 minutes or until apples can be easily pierced with a knife and juices are bubbling. **Yield: 12 servings**

* If apples are very juicy, add an additional ½ tablespoon arrowroot powder.

Per Serving: Fat: 15.4g **Carbs:** 42g **Fiber:** 4.8g **Cal:** 298

Blueberry Cobbler

6 tablespoons xylitol
2 tablespoons arrowroot powder
¼ teaspoon cinnamon
¼ teaspoon nutmeg
4½ cups fresh or frozen blueberries
1 tablespoon freshly squeezed lemon juice
1 tablespoon unsalted butter
Pastry for 9" pie, page 26

Combine xylitol, arrowroot, cinnamon, and nutmeg; add blueberries, stirring until coated. Spoon blueberry mixture into a buttered 8" square baking dish. Sprinkle lemon juice over berries, and dot with butter. Roll pastry out ⅛" thick; trim pastry dough to fit an 8" square baking pan. Place pastry over blueberries, sealing edges to sides of dish. Cut several 1" long slits in crust. Bake at 375° for 25-30 minutes or until pastry is golden brown. **Yield: 9 servings**

Per Serving: **Fat:** 8.3g **Carbs:** 30g **Fiber:** 3.9g **Cal:** 191

Boston Cream Pie

⅓ cup unsalted butter, softened
⅔ cup xylitol
2 eggs, separated
1 teaspoon vanilla extract
1 cup minus 2 tablespoons spelt flour or whole wheat pastry flour
1 teaspoon baking powder
⅛ teaspoon salt
5 tablespoons plain low-fat yogurt
3 tablespoons water
Vanilla Cream Custard Filling, page 64
Chocolate Ganache, page 60

Cream butter and xylitol until light and fluffy. Add egg yolks, one at a time, beating well after each addition. Stir in vanilla extract. Combine flour, baking powder, and salt in small bowl; in another small bowl, combine yogurt and water. Add flour to creamed mixture alternately with yogurt, beginning and ending with flour. Beat egg whites until stiff but not dry; gently fold into cake batter. Pour batter into buttered and floured 9" cake pan. Bake at 350° for 25-30 minutes, or until a toothpick inserted in center comes out clean. Cool in pan 5 minutes, then turn out onto cake rack and cool completely. Slice cake in half horizontally to make 2 layers. Spread one layer with Vanilla Cream Custard, and top with remaining cake layer. Spread Chocolate Ganache over top of cake. Refrigerate until ready to serve. **Yield: 12 servings**

Per Serving: Fat: 17g **Carbs:** 42.9g **Fiber:** 2.3g **Cal:** 301

Chocolate Chiffon Pie

1 envelope unflavored gelatin
1 cup xylitol, divided
½ teaspoon salt
1⅓ cups milk
3 eggs, separated
2 (1½ oz.) maltitol-sweetened dark chocolate bars
1 teaspoon vanilla extract
¼ teaspoon cream of tartar
9" pie shell, baked until done

Combine gelatin, ½ cup xylitol, and salt in a saucepan. In a separate bowl, lightly beat egg yolks; gradually stir milk into yolks. Whisk milk and eggs into mixture in saucepan. Break up chocolate bars and add to mixture. Cook over low heat, whisking constantly until chocolate melts. Continue whisking and cook until mixture is thickened. Remove from heat, and stir in vanilla extract. Transfer to a bowl and refrigerate for 30 minutes.

Meanwhile, beat egg whites and cream of tartar until foamy. Gradually add remaining ½ cup xylitol, and beat until peaks are stiff but not dry. Fold beaten egg whites into chocolate mixture, and pour filling into prepared pie shell. Refrigerate several hours before serving. **Yield: 8 servings**

Per Serving: **Fat:** 14.3g **Carbs:** 38.8g **Fiber:** 3g **Cal:** 291

Chocolate Coconut Pecan Pie

2 tablespoons unsalted butter, melted
½ cup plus 2 tablespoons xylitol
1½ teaspoons vanilla extract
4 (1½ oz.) maltitol-sweetened dark chocolate bars, chopped
2 eggs, slightly beaten
2 tablespoons spelt flour or whole wheat pastry flour
⅓ cup chopped pecans
⅓ cup shredded unsweetened coconut
8½" pie shell

In a saucepan over low heat, combine butter, xylitol, and vanilla. Add chocolate, and stir until chocolate is melted. Stir in eggs and flour, mixing well. Stir in pecans and coconut. Pour mixture into pie shell, and bake at 350° for 30 minutes or until done. Pie puffs during baking and shrinks slightly during cooling. **Yield: 12 servings**

Per Serving: **Fat:** 16g **Carbs:** 21g **Fiber:** 3.4g **Cal:** 245

Key Lime Pie

1 recipe Sweetened Condensed Milk, page 68
4 egg yolks
⅔ cup freshly squeezed lime juice
1 teaspoon finely grated lime zest
1 recipe Italian Meringue, page 27
1 9" graham cracker crumb pie shell, page 27

In a medium bowl, whisk together the sweetened condensed milk and egg yolks. Gradually beat in the lime juice and lime rind. Gently fold 1 cup of the meringue into lime filling, and pour into prepared crust. Bake pie at 350° for 15 minutes. Remove pie from oven and spread remaining meringue over filling, sealing meringue to edge of pastry. Bake pie at 350° for 5 minutes, then broil 1-2 minutes or until meringue is light golden. Cool at room temperature for 30 minutes, then refrigerate for at least 4 hours before serving. **Yield: 10 servings**

Per Serving: Fat: 14g **Carbs:** 61.4g **Fiber:** 1.8g **Cal:** 352

Lemon Ice Box Pie

Follow directions for Key Lime Pie, except substitute lemon juice and lemon zest instead of lime juice and lime zest.

Magnolia Pie

3 eggs
3 tablespoons unsalted butter, melted
1 cup xylitol
2 tablespoons arrowroot powder
1 cup plus 2 tablespoons plain whole milk yogurt
1 teaspoon vanilla extract
½ teaspoon lemon extract
1 teaspoon finely grated lemon zest
9" pie shell, page 26

Beat eggs and butter at medium speed with a mixer until well blended. Add xylitol, arrowroot powder, yogurt, extracts, and lemon zest and mix on low speed until smooth. Pour into pastry shell and bake at 325° for 1 hour or until knife inserted in center comes out clean. **Yield: 10 servings**

Per Serving: Fat: 11.6g **Carbs:** 32g **Fiber:** 1.6g **Cal:** 225

Peanut Butter Pie Squares

8 ounce package reduced-fat cream cheese
12 ounce package firm or extra firm silken tofu
½ cup xylitol
1 teaspoon vanilla extract
½ cup plus 1 tablespoon peanut butter
1 recipe for 9" graham cracker pie shell, page 27

To prepare crust: Prepare recipe for 9" graham cracker pie shell, but press mixture onto bottom and 1" up the sides of an 8" square baking dish. Bake at 375° for 7-8 minutes.

To prepare filling: Place cream cheese and tofu together in food processor or blender, and process until mixture is very smooth. Add xylitol, vanilla extract, and peanut butter, and process again until all ingredients are thoroughly combined. Pour mixture into crust. Refrigerate for several hours or overnight before serving. **Yield: 16 servings**

Per Serving: Fat: 16.2g **Carbs:** 26.6g **Fiber:** 3.5g **Cal:** 263

Pecan Pie Squares

4 egg yolks
4 tablespoons unsalted butter
1 cup minus 2 tablespoons xylitol
2 tablespoons reduced-fat sour cream
2 tablespoons plain whole milk yogurt
¼ teaspoon salt
1 teaspoon vanilla extract
½ teaspoon maple flavoring
1 cup pecan halves
¼ cup finely chopped pecans
1 recipe for 9" pie shell, page 26

To prepare crust: Prepare recipe for 9" pie shell, but roll and cut pastry to cover bottom and 1" up the sides of an 8" square baking dish. Pre-bake crust as directed on page xiv.

To prepare filling: Place the pecans, flat sides down, in the bottom of the pie shell. In a saucepan, combine the egg yolks, butter, xylitol, sour cream, yogurt, and salt. Cook over low heat, stirring constantly, for 8-10 minutes or until mixture begins to thicken. Stir in vanilla extract, maple flavoring, and finely chopped pecans. Pour the filling over the pecans in the pie shell, and bake at 350° for 20-25 minutes or until filling puffs up and begins to bubble around edges. Allow to cool before serving. **Yield: 16 servings**

Per Serving: Fat: 14.2g **Carbs:** 18.8g **Fiber:** 1.6g **Cal:** 195

Pumpkin Pie

    2 eggs
    1¾ cups canned pumpkin
    ¾ cup xylitol
    ⅛ teaspoon salt
    ⅛ teaspoon cloves
    ¼ teaspoon ginger
    ¼ teaspoon nutmeg
    1½ teaspoons cinnamon
    1 cup plain whole milk yogurt
    9" pie shell, page 26

In large mixing bowl, lightly beat eggs. Add pumpkin and mix well. Stir in xylitol, salt, and spices until thoroughly combined. Gradually stir in yogurt. Pour filling into pie crust. Bake at 375° for 50-60 minutes, or until knife inserted in center comes out clean. Serve chilled with whipped cream and a sprinkle of cinnamon. Delicious! **Yield: 8 servings**

Note: Mixing the pumpkin filling in the food processor creates an exceptionally smooth and silky texture.

Per Serving: Fat: 9.8g **Carbs:** 36.3g **Fiber:** 4.2g **Cal:** 229

Southern Sweet Potato Cream Pie

    3 cups cooked, mashed sweet potatoes
    2 tablespoons unsalted butter, softened
    2 tablespoons lecithin granules
    ½ cup plus 1 tablespoon xylitol
    1 teaspoon cinnamon
    ¾ teaspoon nutmeg
    ½ teaspoon lemon extract
    1½ teaspoons vanilla extract
    3 eggs
    ¾ cup plain whole milk yogurt
    ¼ cup water
    10" pie shell, page 26

In a large bowl, beat sweet potatoes, butter, lecithin, xylitol, spices, extracts, and eggs until mixture is smooth. Combine yogurt and water in a small bowl. Gradually add yogurt into sweet potato mixture, beating until well blended. Pour filling into pie shell. Bake at 375° for 40 minutes or until knife inserted in center comes out clean. Allow pie to cool completely before serving. **Yield: 10 servings**

Per Servings: Fat: 13g **Carbs:** 40g **Fiber:** 4g **Cal:** 286

Pie Crust – 9"

1 cup spelt flour or whole wheat pastry flour
¼ teaspoon salt
5 tablespoons unsalted butter, cut into small pieces
1-3 tablespoons ice water

Hand Mixing: Combine flour and salt in large bowl. Cut butter in until mixture is texture of coarse meal. Sprinkle 1 tablespoon of water at a time over flour mixture, mix lightly with a fork after each addition, until pastry is just moist enough to hold together when pressed between fingers. Shape the pastry into a flattened disc about ½ inch think, cover with plastic wrap, and chill for 30 minutes. Roll pastry out between two sheets of wax paper until pastry is desired size. Refrigerate briefly; remove wax paper and fit pastry into pie plate. **Yield: pastry for one 9" pie shell or 8 servings**

Food Processor Method: Place flour and salt in food processor. Using the metal blade, pulse on and off a few times to combine mixture well. Remove lid and distribute pieces of butter evenly into bowl. Replace lid, and pulse several times or until texture of mixture resembles coarse meal. Add 1 tablespoon of water at a time through feed tube, and pulse several times after each addition until pastry holds together when pressed between fingers. Shape pastry into a flattened disc, cover with plastic wrap, and chill for 30 minutes. Roll pastry out between two sheets of wax paper until pastry is desired size. Refrigerate briefly; remove wax paper and fit pastry into pie plate.

Note: See page xiv for baking directions.

Per Serving: Fat: 7.4g **Carbs:** 12.5g **Fiber:** 2g **Cal:** 128

Pie Crust – 10"

1⅓ cups spelt flour or whole wheat pastry flour
6 tablespoons plus 2 teaspoons unsalted butter
⅜ teaspoon salt
2-3 tablespoons ice water

Follow above directions for preparing pie crust. **Yield: pastry for one 10" pie shell or 10 servings**

Note: See page xiv for baking directions.

Per Serving: Fat: 7.8g **Carbs:** 13.3g **Fiber:** 2.1g **Cal:** 136

Graham Cracker Crust

  1½ cups graham cracker crumbs
  ¼ cup xylitol
  4 tablespoons unsalted butter, melted

Combine graham cracker crumbs, xylitol, and melted butter; mix well. Press mixture onto the bottom and side of the pie plate. Bake at 375° for 7-8 minutes. **Yield: one 9" pie shell or 10 servings**

Note: This recipe may also be used as a crust for cheesecakes. Press mixture into the bottom and 1½" up the sides of the springform pan. Baking temperature and time is the same as above.

Per Serving: Fat: 7.5g **Carbs:** 25.5g **Fiber:** 1.8g **Cal:** 169

Italian Meringue

  ½ cup xylitol
  2 tablespoons water
  4 egg whites
  ½ teaspoon cream of tartar

In a small nonstick saucepan, combine xylitol and water and stir well. Cook over medium heat, stirring constantly, until xylitol dissolves and mixture is bubbly. Remove from heat. In another bowl, beat egg whites until foamy. Add cream of tartar and beat until stiff peaks form. Return saucepan to heat, and cook to 236° (soft ball stage). Immediately begin pouring mixture in a steady stream into beaten egg whites, while beating, and continue beating until bowl is no longer hot and stiff peaks are formed. Spread meringue over pie filling, and bake at 350° for 5 minutes, then broil for 1-2 minutes or until meringue is light golden. **Yield: 10 servings on Key Lime and Lemon Ice Box Pies**

Per Serving: Fat: 0g **Carbs:** 9.7g **Fiber:** 0g **Cal:** 31

Cheesecakes

Almond-Flavored Cheesecake

Crust:
- 5 tablespoons unsalted butter
- 4½ tablespoons xylitol
- 1 cup spelt flour or whole wheat pastry flour
- ¼ teaspoon salt
- ¼ cup finely chopped pecans

Filling:
- 1 cup low-fat cottage cheese
- 2 (8 oz.) packages reduced-fat cream cheese, softened
- ¾ cup xylitol
- 3 eggs
- ¾ teaspoon vanilla extract
- ¾ teaspoon almond extract
- 1 cup reduced-fat sour cream
- 1 cup low-fat plain yogurt

To prepare crust: Cream butter and xylitol together until light and fluffy. Stir in flour, salt, and pecans. Spread half of dough evenly in bottom of 9" springform pan. Bake at 350° for 10-12 minutes, or until very light golden. Remove from oven, and allow to cool. Attach sides to springform pan, and press remaining dough from bottom 1" up sides of springform pan.

To prepare filling: Process cottage cheese in blender or food processor until smooth and creamy. Beat cream cheese and xylitol together until light and fluffy; blend in creamed cottage cheese. Add eggs, one at a time, beating until just blended. Stir in extracts. Combine sour cream and yogurt; gently fold into cream cheese mixture.

To bake cheesecake: Pour into springform pan, and bake in a waterbath (see page xv) at 325° for 50 minutes. Turn oven off and prop oven door open; leave cheesecake in oven another 30 minutes. Remove cheesecake from waterbath, allow to sit at room temperature for 30 minutes, then refrigerate for at least 8 hours or until thoroughly chilled. Carefully remove sides of pan, loosen cheesecake from bottom of pan, and slide cheesecake onto a serving plate. **Yield: 16 servings**

Variation: After pouring cheesecake batter into pan, but before baking cheesecake, spoon ½ cup strawberry, blueberry, or raspberry puree (or fruit spread) over batter, and swirl lightly with a knife to create a marbled effect. Bake as directed above.

Per Serving: Fat: 12.3g **Carbs:** 23.8g **Fiber:** 1.1g **Cal:** 218

Cherry Cheesecake

Almond Pastry:
- 5 tablespoons xylitol
- 5 tablespoons unsalted butter
- 1 cup spelt flour or whole wheat pastry flour
- ¼ teaspoon salt
- ¼ cup ground almonds

Filling:
- 1 cup low-fat cottage cheese
- 2 (8 oz.) packages reduced-fat cream cheese, softened
- 1 cup xylitol
- ⅛ teaspoon salt
- 3 eggs
- 1¾ teaspoon cherry flavoring
- ⅓ cup low-fat plain yogurt
- 3 tablespoons reduced-fat sour cream
- ⅓ cup finely chopped dried cherries that have marinated in 3 tablespoons cherry liqueur for 1 hour or until cherries have absorbed all the liqueur

To prepare crust: Cream together butter and xylitol until light and fluffy. Stir in flour, salt, and almonds. Press half of dough onto bottom of 9" springform pan (sides removed). Bake at 350° for 10-12 minutes or until very light golden. Remove from oven, and allow to cool. Attach sides to bottom of pan, and press remaining dough from bottom of pan 1" up sides of pan.

To prepare filling: Process cottage cheese in blender or food processor until smooth and creamy. Beat cream cheese and xylitol until light and fluffy; blend in creamed cottage cheese and salt. Add eggs, one at a time, beating until just blended. Gently fold in yogurt, sour cream, and cherries.

To bake cheesecake: Pour batter into springform pan, and bake in a waterbath (see page xv) at 325° for 50 minutes. Turn oven off and prop oven door open; leave cheesecake in oven another 30 minutes. Remove cheesecake from waterbath, allow to sit at room temperature for 30 minutes, then refrigerate for at least 8 hours or until thoroughly chilled. Carefully remove sides of pan, loosen cheesecake from bottom of pan, and slide cheesecake onto a serving plate. **Yield: 16 servings**

Per Serving: Fat: 11.1g **Carbs:** 29g **Fiber:** 1.4g **Cal:** 228

Grasshopper Cheesecake

Crust:
⅓ recipe (approx.) of Chocolate Cookies, page 41

Filling:
1 cup low-fat cottage cheese
2 (8 oz.) packages reduced-fat cream cheese, softened
¾ cup plus 2 tablespoons xylitol
3 eggs
2½ tablespoons crème de cacao
2½ tablespoons crème de menthe
1½ teaspoons vanilla extract
3 tablespoons plain low-fat yogurt
3 tablespoons reduced-fat sour cream

To prepare crust: Press cookie dough onto bottom and 1" up sides of 9" springform pan. Bake at 350° for 8-10 minutes.

To prepare filling: Process cottage cheese in blender or food processor until smooth and creamy. Beat cream cheese and xylitol at high speed until light and fluffy; blend in creamed cottage cheese. Add eggs, one at a time, beating until just blended. Combine liqueurs and vanilla extract, and stir into filling. Combine yogurt and sour cream; gently fold into cream cheese mixture.

To bake cheesecake: Pour into springform pan, and bake in a waterbath (see page xv) at 325° for 50 minutes. Turn off oven and prop oven door open; leave cheesecake in oven another 30 minutes. Remove cheesecake from waterbath, allow to sit at room temperature for 30 minutes, then refrigerate for at least 8 hours or until thoroughly chilled. Carefully remove sides of pan, loosen cheesecake from bottom of pan, and slide cheesecake onto a serving plate. **Yield: 16 servings**

Per Serving: Fat: 7.6g **Carbs:** 21.6g **Fiber:** 0g **Cal:** 170

Lemon Cheesecake

Crust:
- 5 tablespoons unsalted butter
- 4 tablespoons xylitol
- 1 cup spelt flour or whole wheat pastry flour
- ¼ teaspoon salt
- 1 teaspoon grated lemon zest

Filling:
- 1 cup low-fat cottage cheese
- 2 (8 oz.) packages reduced-fat cream cheese, softened
- 1 cup xylitol
- ⅛ teaspoon salt
- 3 eggs
- ½ teaspoon lemon extract
- 1 teaspoon finely grated lemon zest
- ¼ cup low-fat plain yogurt
- ¼ cup reduced-fat sour cream

To prepare crust: Cream butter and xylitol together until light and fluffy. Stir in flour, salt, and lemon zest. Spread half of dough evenly in bottom of 9" springform pan (sides removed). Bake at 350° for 10-12 minutes, or until very light golden. Remove from oven, and allow to cool. Attach sides to springform pan, and press remaining dough from bottom 1" up sides of pan.

To prepare filling: Process cottage cheese in blender or food processor until smooth and creamy. Beat cream cheese and xylitol together until light and fluffy; blend in creamed cottage cheese and salt. Add eggs, one at a time, beating until just blended. Stir in lemon extract and lemon zest; mix well. Combine yogurt and sour cream; gently fold into cream cheese mixture.

To bake cheesecake: Pour into springform pan, and bake in a waterbath (see page xv) at 325° for 50 minutes. Turn oven off and prop oven door open; leave cheesecake in oven another 30 minutes. Remove cheesecake from waterbath, allow to sit at room temperature for 30 minutes, then refrigerate for at least 8 hours or until thoroughly chilled. Carefully remove sides of pan, loosen cheesecake from bottom of pan, and slide cheesecake onto a serving plate. **Yield: 16 servings**

Per Serving: Fat: 10g **Carbs:** 24.4g **Fiber:** 1g **Cal:** 194

Orange Cheesecake

Crust:
- 1½ cups graham cracker crumbs
- ¼ cup xylitol
- 4 tablespoons unsalted butter, melted

Filling:
- 1 cup low-fat cottage cheese
- 2 (8 oz.) packages reduced-fat cream cheese, softened
- 1 cup xylitol
- 3 eggs
- 1 tablespoon orange zest
- 2 tablespoons Triple Sec Orange Liqueur
- ¼ teaspoon orange extract
- ¼ cup low-fat plain yogurt
- ¼ cup reduced-fat sour cream

To prepare crust: Combine graham cracker crumbs, xylitol, and butter; mix well. Press onto bottom and 1" up sides of 9" springform pan. Bake at 375° for 7-8 minutes. Remove from oven and allow to cool.

To prepare filling: Process cottage cheese in blender or food processor until smooth and creamy. Beat cream cheese and xylitol until light and fluffy; blend in creamed cottage cheese. Add eggs, one at a time, beating until just blended. Stir in orange zest, liqueur, and extract. Combine yogurt and sour cream; gently fold into cream cheese mixture.

To bake cheesecake: Pour filling into springform pan, and bake in a waterbath (see page xv) at 325° for 50 minutes. Turn off oven and prop oven door open; leave cheesecake in oven another 30 minutes. Remove cheesecake from waterbath, and allow to sit at room temperature for 30 minutes, then refrigerate for at least 8 hours or until thoroughly chilled. Carefully remove sides of pan, loosen cheesecake from bottom of pan, and slide cheesecake onto a serving plate. **Yield: 16 servings**

Per Serving: Fat: 11.2g **Carbs:** 32g **Fiber:** 1.1g **Cal:** 236

Pumpkin Cheesecake

Crust:
- 1½ cups graham cracker crumbs
- ¼ cup xylitol
- 4 tablespoons unsalted butter, melted

Filling:
- 1 cup low-fat cottage cheese
- 2 (8 oz.) packages reduced-fat cream cheese, softened
- ¾ cup plus 2 tablespoons xylitol
- 3 eggs
- 1 egg yolk
- ½ teaspoon allspice
- ½ teaspoon ginger
- ½ teaspoon cinnamon
- ¼ teaspoon salt
- 1 cup plus 2 tablespoons canned pumpkin
- ⅓ cup reduced-fat sour cream
- ⅓ cup low-fat plain yogurt
- 1 teaspoon vanilla extract

To prepare crust: Combine graham cracker crumbs, xylitol, and butter; mix well. Press onto bottom and 1" up sides of 9" springform pan. Bake at 375° for 7-8 minutes. Remove from oven, and allow to cool.

To prepare filling: Process cottage cheese in blender or food processor until smooth and creamy. Beat cream cheese and xylitol until light and fluffy; blend in creamed cottage cheese. Add eggs, one at a time, beating until just blended. Combine allspice, ginger, cinnamon, and salt; add to cream cheese mixture and mix well. Add pumpkin, sour cream, yogurt, and vanilla; mix until well blended.

To bake cheesecake: Pour filling into springform pan, and bake in waterbath (see page xv) at 325° for 50 minutes. Turn oven off and prop oven door open; leave cheesecake in oven another 30 minutes. Remove cheesecake from waterbath, allow to sit at room temperature for 30 minutes, then refrigerate for at least 8 hours or until thoroughly chilled. Carefully remove sides of pan, loosen cheesecake from bottom of pan, and slide cheesecake onto a serving plate. **Yield: 16 servings**

Per Servings: Fat: 11.7g **Carbs:** 31.1g **Fiber:** 1.8g **Cal:** 236

Cookies

Apple Oatmeal Bars

1 cup spelt flour or whole wheat pastry flour
½ teaspoon baking soda
⅔ cup xylitol, divided
1 cup quick-cooking oats
4 tablespoons unsalted butter
3 tablespoons unsweetened applesauce
3 medium apples, cored and thinly sliced (no need to peel apples)
1 scant tablespoon unsalted butter
1 teaspoon cinnamon

Combine flour, baking soda, ⅓ cup xylitol, and oats. Cut in butter, and stir in applesauce. Mixture should be crumbly. Spoon half this mixture into bottom of buttered 7½" x 12" glass baking dish. Gently press mixture evenly into baking dish. Arrange apple slices over crust, and dot with butter. Mix ⅓ cup xylitol and cinnamon together, and sprinkle over apples. Spoon remaining crust mixture over apples. Cover dish with wax paper and press down firmly, then remove wax paper and bake at 350° for 30-35 minutes or until topping is golden brown and apples are easily pierced with a knife. **Yield: 18 servings**

Per Serving: Fat: 3.7g **Carbs:** 19.9g **Fiber:** 2.4g **Cal:** 110

Chocolate Chip Coconut Bars

1½ cups graham cracker crumbs
4 tablespoons unsalted butter
3 tablespoons xylitol
⅔ cup shredded coconut
1 cup chopped pecans
1 recipe sweetened condensed milk, page 68
4 (1.5 oz. each) maltitol-sweetened dark chocolate bars, chopped

Combine graham cracker crumbs, butter and xylitol. Press into bottom of buttered 9" x 13" pan. Bake at 375° for 7 minutes. Watch closely, this can overcook easily. Combine coconut, pecans, and sweetened condensed milk, and pour over crust. Sprinkle chocolate evenly over top of bars. Gently press chocolate onto filling using back of spoon. Bake at 350° for 20-25 minutes. Center will be soft, but will become more firm as bars cool. **Yield: 36 servings**

Per Serving: Fat: 8.2g **Carbs:** 14.7g **Fiber:** 1.4g **Cal:** 134

Chocolate Chip Cookies

¼ cup unsalted butter
2 tablespoons unsweetened applesauce
¾ cup xylitol
1 egg
1 teaspoon vanilla extract
1 cup plus 2 tablespoons spelt flour or whole wheat pastry flour
½ teaspoon baking soda
¼ teaspoon salt
4 oz. maltitol-sweetened dark chocolate bars, chopped

In large bowl, cream butter with xylitol until fluffy. Gradually add applesauce into mixture during creaming process. Beat in egg and vanilla extract. In another bowl, combine flour, baking soda, and salt. Gradually stir flour mixture into batter, and fold in chocolate. Drop by rounded teaspoonfuls onto parchment-lined cookie sheet. Bake at 350° for 10-12 minutes or until golden brown. Cookies are soft when taken from the oven, but they become more firm when stored overnight in an airtight container. **Yield: 2½ dozen cookies**

Per Cookie: **Fat:** 3.1g **Carbs:** 8.8g **Fiber:** 1g **Cal:** 65

For White Chocolate Macadamia Nut Cookies

Follow above directions for Chocolate Chip Cookies except:

Substitute 3 ounces maltitol-sweetened white chocolate bars for the dark chocolate, and add ⅔ cup chopped macadamia nuts to the batter before baking the cookies. Allow cookies to cool a few minutes before removing them from the cookie sheet. Cool on wax paper-lined racks. **Yield: 3 dozen cookies**

Per Cookie: **Fat:** 4.2g **Carbs:** 7.8g **Fiber:** 0.8g **Cal:** 69

Chocolate Coconut Brownies

2 tablespoons unsalted butter
4 (1½ oz.) maltitol-sweetened dark chocolate bars
½ cup plus 1 tablespoon xylitol
1½ teaspoon vanilla extract
3 eggs, beaten
¼ cup spelt flour or whole wheat pastry flour
⅓ cup shredded coconut
⅓ cup chopped pecans

In saucepan, over low heat, melt butter. Break bars into pieces and add to butter. Stir in xylitol and vanilla extract. Continue cooking over low heat, stirring frequently, until chocolate is completely melted. Remove from heat and stir in eggs until thoroughly combined with chocolate mixture. Stir in flour, coconut and pecans. Pour mixture into buttered 8" square pan and bake at 350° for 25-30 minutes or until outer edges are somewhat firm. Center will still be soft, but will become more firm as brownies cool. Allow brownies to cool completely before cutting. **Yield: 25 brownies**

Note: This makes a moist, rich sweet brownie.

Per Brownie: Fat: 5.7g **Carbs:** 6.1g **Fiber:** 1.1g **Cal:** 81

For Chocolate Cherry Brownies

Follow above directions for Chocolate Coconut Brownies except:

Delete the coconut and the pecans. Instead, add ⅓ cup of finely chopped dried cherries that have marinated in 3 tbsp. cherry liqueur for several hours or overnight. Drain any excess liquor before adding cherries to the brownie batter. Substitute 1½ tsp. cherry flavoring for the vanilla extract. **Yield: 25 brownies**

Per Brownie: Fat: 3.9g **Carbs:** 7.9g **Fiber:** 0.9g **Cal:** 77

Chocolate Cookies

4 tablespoons unsalted butter
¾ cup xylitol
2 tablespoons unsweetened applesauce
1 egg
1 teaspoon vanilla extract
1¼ cups spelt flour or whole wheat pastry flour
¼ cup unsweetened cocoa powder
¾ teaspoon baking soda
¼ teaspoon salt

Cream butter and xylitol until light and fluffy; gradually add applesauce during the creaming process. Beat in egg and vanilla extract. Combine flour, cocoa powder, baking soda, and salt. Stir in flour mixture, a little at a time, until all ingredients are well mixed. Cover bowl and place in freezer for 1 hour or until dough is firm enough to easily handle. Measure 1 level teaspoon of dough. Roll into ball and place on parchment lined cookie sheet. Flatten to 1½" diameter. Bake cookies at 375° for 4-5 minutes. Cookies will puff up, then go down slightly. Remove them from oven before they brown around the edges. **Yield: 5 dozen cookies**

Per Cookie: Fat: 0.9g **Carbs:** 4.8g **Fiber:** 0.4g **Cal:** 26

For Chocolate Sandwich Cookies:

The Chocolate Cookies above are delicious just as they are, or they can be filled with a variety of cream fillings – Cherry Filling, Crème de Menthe Filling, Lemon Filling, or Orange Filling – on page 48. **Yield: 2½ dozen sandwich cookies**

Chocolate Pecan Pie Bars

Crust:
- 1½ cups spelt flour or whole wheat pastry flour
- ¼ cup xylitol
- ¼ teaspoon salt
- 5 tablespoons unsalted butter
- 4 tablespoons plain whole milk yogurt

Filling:
- 4 (1½ oz.) maltitol-sweetened dark chocolate bars, chopped
- 2 tablespoons water
- 1 cup xylitol
- 1 tablespoon lecithin granules
- 4 eggs, slightly beaten
- 1½ teaspoons vanilla extract
- 2 cup slightly chopped pecans

To make crust: Mix flour, xylitol, and salt together, then cut in butter until mixture resembles coarse crumbs. Stir in yogurt and form into ball. Butter bottom and sides of 7½" x 12" glass baking dish. Roll dough out between two sheets of wax paper to size that is 2" wider and longer than bottom of baking dish. Fit dough into pan and bake at 350° for 20 minutes.

To make filling: In medium saucepan, over low heat, warm chocolate in water until chocolate pieces are completely melted. Stir in xylitol and lecithin. Remove pan from heat and add eggs and vanilla extract, stirring until well blended. Stir in pecans. Pour filling over crust and spread evenly. Bake at 350° for 30 minutes or until filling is firm around edges and center is slightly soft. Allow to cool in pan before cutting into bars. **Yield: 48 bars**

Per Bar: **Fat:** 6.4g **Carbs:** 9.3g **Fiber:** 1.2g **Cal:** 96

Lemon Pecan Cookies

½ cup unsalted butter
⅔ cup xylitol
4 tablespoons unsweetened applesauce
1 tablespoon grated lemon zest
1 tablespoon lemon juice
½ teaspoon lemon extract
2¼ cups spelt flour or whole wheat pastry flour
¼ teaspoon salt
½ cup finely chopped pecans

Cream butter and xylitol until light and fluffy, gradually add applesauce during creaming process. Stir in lemon zest, juice, and extract. Combine flour and salt, and gradually stir into creamed mixture. Cover and refrigerate for 1 hour or until dough is firm enough to easily handle. Roll dough into 1" diameter balls, and then roll in pecans. Place on parchment lined cookie sheet. Press down lightly with thin spatula. Bake at 350° for 10-12 minutes or until underside of cookies is light brown. **Yield: 4½ dozen cookies**

Per Cookie: Fat: 2.5g **Carbs:** 6.9g **Fiber:** 0.8g **Cal:** 50

Peanut Butter Cookies

4 tablespoons unsalted butter
1 cup xylitol
1 tablespoon prune puree, page 69
1 tablespoon plain non-fat yogurt
½ cup peanut butter
1 egg

1¼ cups spelt flour or whole
   wheat pastry flour
1 teaspoon baking soda
¼ teaspoon salt
½ teaspoon vanilla extract

Cream butter and xylitol until light and fluffy; gradually add prune puree and yogurt during creaming process. Beat in peanut butter and egg. In small bowl, combine flour, baking soda, and salt. Stir dry ingredients into creamed mixture. Cover and refrigerate for 1 hour or until dough can be handled easily. Roll into balls, using ½ tablespoon of dough per cookie. Place on parchment paper-lined cookie sheet. Flatten cookies with a fork dipped in flour to create a criss-cross pattern. Bake at 350° for 8-10 minutes or until outer edges of cookies are light brown. **Yield: 5 dozen cookies**

Note: Cookies are soft after baking. Allow them to cool completely, then store in an airtight container overnight. The next day they will be much more firm.

Per Cookie: **Fat:** 2g **Carbs:** 5.9g **Fiber:** 0.6g **Cal:** 41

Raisin Spice Cookies

4 tablespoons unsalted butter
¾ cup xylitol
2 tablespoons unsweetened applesauce
2 eggs
1½ cups spelt flour or whole wheat
   pastry flour
1½ teaspoon baking powder

1 teaspoon cinnamon
½ teaspoon nutmeg
¼ teaspoon cloves
½ teaspoon salt
⅔ cup raisins
⅓ cup chopped pecans

Rehydrate raisins by covering them with warm water and allowing to soak for at least 30 minutes. Cream butter and xylitol; gradually add applesauce during creaming process. Beat in eggs. Combine flour, baking powder, spices, and salt. Blend flour mixture into creamed ingredients. Drain water from raisins and stir raisins and pecans into batter. Drop teaspoonfuls of batter onto parchment lined cookie sheet. Bake at 325° for 12-15 minutes or until light brown. **Yield: 4 dozen cookies**

Per Cookie: **Fat:** 1.8g **Carbs:** 8.1g **Fiber:** 0.7g **Cal:** 48

Thumbprint Cookies

4 tablespoons unsalted butter
⅓ cup xylitol
2 tablespoons unsweetened applesauce
1 egg yolk
½ teaspoon vanilla extract
1 cup spelt flour or whole wheat pastry flour
¼ teaspoon salt
½ cup finely chopped pecans
2 tablespoons fruit spread or jam

Cream butter and xylitol until light and fluffy; gradually add applesauce during creaming process. Beat in egg yolk and vanilla extract. Combine flour and salt in a small bowl, and stir into creamed mixture. Form dough into ball, wrap in plastic wrap, and chill in refrigerator for 1 hour or until dough is easily handled.

Roll dough into 1" balls. Roll in chopped pecans. Place on a parchment lined cookie sheet, and press an indentation into each cookie with your thumb or a very small rounded measuring spoon. Fill each indentation with fruit spread. Bake at 375° for 10-12 minutes or until bottom of cookies are light brown. **Yield: 3 dozen cookies**

Per Cookie: **Fat:** 2.6g **Carbs:** 5.4g **Fiber:** 0.6g **Cal:** 45

Tropical Fruit Bars

1 cup dates, chopped
20 ounce can unsweetened crushed pineapple with juice
1 cup spelt flour or whole wheat pastry flour
⅔ cup unsweetened, shredded coconut
½ cup chopped pecans
3 cups quick-cooking oats
¼ cup xylitol
1 tablespoon lecithin granules
1 cup freshly squeezed orange juice
2 tablespoons extra virgin olive oil
2 tablespoons unsweetened applesauce

Combine the dates and pineapple with its juice in a saucepan. Cook on medium-low heat until fruit mixture is thick, stirring occasionally, and set aside. In a large bowl, combine flour, coconut, pecans, oats, xylitol, and lecithin granules. In a small bowl, mix orange juice, oil, and apple-sauce. Add to the oat mixture and mix well. Press half of this mixture into a buttered 9" x 13" pan. Spread fruit evenly on top of crust. Roll out remaining dough between 2 sheets of wax paper to 9" x 13". Place top crust over fruit mixture, and press lightly. Bake at 325° for 25-30 minutes or until top crust is light brown. **Yield: 36 bars**

Per Bar: **Fat:** 3.7g **Carbs:** 16.8g **Fiber:** 2.4g **Cal:** 93

Vanilla Sandwich Creams

½ cup unsalted butter
½ cup xylitol
4 tablespoons unsweetened applesauce
1 teaspoon vanilla extract
1¾ cups spelt flour or whole wheat pastry flour
¼ teaspoon salt

Cream butter and xylitol until light and fluffy; gradually beat in applesauce. Stir in vanilla extract. In a medium bowl, combine flour and salt. Stir flour into creamed mixture. Cover and refrigerate for 1 hour or until dough can be handled easily. Shape dough into balls, using ½ tablespoon of dough for each. Place on parchment paper-lined cookie sheet. Flatten cookie slightly with the bottom of a glass that has been dipped in flour. Bake at 400° for 8-10 minutes or until edges are very lightly browned. Put cookies together in pairs with one of the fillings listed on page 48. **Yield: 27 sandwich cookies**

Per Sandwich Cookie: Fat: 4.7g **Carbs:** 16.3g **Fiber:** 0.8g **Cal:** 97

Fillings For Sandwich Cookies

Cherry Filling

3 tablespoons unsalted butter
1 cup powdered xylitol
4 teaspoons milk (or water)

⅓ cup dry milk powder
¾ teaspoon cherry flavoring

Whip butter until light; gradually beat in xylitol and dry milk powder, adding milk (or water) as needed, until mixture is smooth and correct consistency. Stir in cherry flavoring.

Filling Per Sandwich Cookie: **Fat:** 1.1g **Carbs:** 6.8g **Fiber:** 0g **Cal:** 29

Crème de Menthe Filling

½ cup unsalted butter
½ cup minus 1 tablespoon dry milk powder
4 tablespoons xylitol
4 teaspoons crème de menthe

Whip butter until light; gradually beat in milk powder and xylitol until mixture is smooth. Stir in crème de menthe.

Filling Per Sandwich Cookie: **Fat:** 2.9g **Carbs:** 2.4g **Fiber:** 0g **Cal:** 137

Lemon Filling

3 tablespoons unsalted butter
1 cup powdered xylitol
⅓ cup dry milk powder
2 teaspoons fresh lemon juice

2 teaspoons water
⅜ teaspoon lemon extract
1½ teaspoons finely grated
 lemon zest

Whip butter until light; gradually beat in xylitol and dry milk powder, adding lemon juice and water as needed, until mixture is smooth and correct consistency. Stir in lemon extract and lemon zest.

Filling Per Sandwich Cookie: **Fat:** 1.1g **Carbs:** 6.8g **Fiber:** 0g **Cal:** 29

Orange Filling

Follow above directions for Lemon Filling, except substitute fresh orange juice for lemon juice, orange extract for lemon extract, and orange zest for lemon zest.

Filling Per Sandwich Cookie: **Fat:** 1.1g **Carbs:** 6.8g **Fiber:** 0g **Cal:** 29

Breads
and
Muffins

Blueberry Lemon Pecan Scones

1½ cup plus 2 tablespoons spelt flour or whole wheat pastry flour
¼ cup plus 1 teaspoon xylitol
1 teaspoon baking powder
½ teaspoon baking soda
4 tablespoons unsalted butter, cut into small pieces
½ cup plain low-fat yogurt
1½ teaspoons finely grated lemon zest
⅓ cup unsweetened applesauce
⅔ cup blueberries, frozen
¼ cup finely chopped pecans

Thoroughly combine flour, xylitol, baking powder, and baking soda. Cut in butter until mixture resembles fine crumbs. Stir in pecans, lemon zest, and blueberries. Combine applesauce and yogurt and stir into flour mixture just until dry ingredients are evenly moistened.

Line a baking sheet with parchment paper, and lightly oil the top of the paper. Transfer the dough to the paper. Lightly flour hands and shape the dough into a 7" diameter round. Using a sharp knife that has been floured, cut the round into 8 wedges.

Bake scones in a preheated oven at 350° for 25 minutes or until lightly browned. These scones are best when served immediately after baking. **Yield: 8 servings**

Per Scone: Fat: 9.1g **Carbs:** 30.8g **Fiber:** 4g **Cal:** 214

Blueberry Muffins

2 cups spelt flour or whole wheat pastry flour
¾ cup plus 1 tablespoon xylitol
2 teaspoons baking powder
⅛ teaspoon salt
1½ teaspoons finely grated lemon zest
1½ cups fresh or frozen blueberries
2 eggs
1 cup plain low-fat yogurt
2 tablespoons water
2 tablespoons extra virgin olive oil
1½ tablespoons unsweetened applesauce

In medium bowl, combine flour, xylitol, baking powder, salt, and lemon zest. Gently stir blueberries into flour mixture until berries are coated with flour. In another bowl, mix eggs, yogurt, water, oil, and applesauce. Add liquid mixture to dry ingredients all at once, and stir just until flour is moistened. Coat inside of muffin cups with nonstick spray. Spoon batter into muffin pan and bake at 375° for 20 minutes or until muffins are light golden and toothpick inserted in center comes out clean. **Yield: 14 muffins**

Per Muffin: **Fat:** 3.6g **Carbs:** 28.5g **Fiber:** 2.8g **Cal:** 148

Carrot Spice Muffins

1 cup spelt flour or whole wheat pastry flour
½ cup quick-cooking oats
1 teaspoon baking soda
½ teaspoon baking powder
½ teaspoon cinnamon
¼ teaspoon nutmeg
⅛ teaspoon ginger
⅛ teaspoon allspice
⅓ cup xylitol
1 egg
¾ cup plain low-fat yogurt
2 tablespoons extra-virgin olive oil
2 tablespoons unsweetened applesauce
½ teaspoon vanilla extract
1½ cups finely grated carrots
½ cup raisins (optional)

Mix flour, oats, baking soda, baking powder, spices, and xylitol in a large bowl. In a medium bowl, mix together egg, yogurt, oil, applesauce, vanilla, carrots, and raisins. Add liquid ingredients all at once to flour mixture, and stir just until flour is moistened. Coat muffin pan cups with nonstick spray. Spoon batter into muffin pan and bake at 375° for 15 minutes or until toothpick inserted in center comes out clean. **Yield: 12 muffins**

Per Muffin: Fat: 3.6g **Carbs:** 18.6g **Fiber:** 2.4g **Cal:** 108

Chocolate Chip Orange Muffins

1½ cups spelt flour or whole wheat pastry flour
½ cup xylitol
2 teaspoons baking powder
¼ teaspoon salt
1 egg
½ cup plain low-fat yogurt
2 tablespoons unsweetened applesauce
2 tablespoons extra-virgin olive oil
2 (1.5 ounces each) maltitol-sweetened dark chocolate bars, chopped
2 tablespoons freshly grated orange zest

Combine flour, xylitol, baking powder, salt, chocolate, and orange zest in a medium size bowl. In another bowl, mix together egg, yogurt, applesauce, and oil. Add the liquid ingredients all at once to the flour mixture, and stir just until flour is moistened. Coat muffin cups with non-stick spray. Spoon batter into muffin pan and bake in oven at 400° for 15 minutes, or until toothpick inserted in center of muffin comes out clean. **Yield: 8 muffins**

Note: The combination of chocolate and orange flavors makes these muffins absolutely delicious.

Per Muffin: Fat: 8.8g **Carbs:** 32.2g **Fiber:** 4.1g **Cal:** 225

Date Orange Bread

½ cup boiling water
¾ cup xylitol
⅓ cup freshly squeezed orange juice
2 tablespoons extra virgin olive oil
1 egg
1½ teaspoons lecithin granules
¼ teaspoon baking soda
2 teaspoons baking powder
¼ teaspoon salt
1½ cup spelt flour or whole wheat pastry flour
2 tablespoons freshly grated orange zest
1 cup chopped dates

Combine boiling water and xylitol, and stir until xylitol is dissolved.
Add orange juice, oil, and egg and mix together thoroughly. Combine
lecithin, baking soda, baking powder, salt, flour, orange zest, and dates.
Gradually add the flour mixture to the liquid ingredients, stirring well
between additions of flour. Pour into buttered 9"x 5"x 3" loaf pan and
bake at 350° for 40-45 minutes or until toothpick inserted in center
comes out clean. Cover with foil, if needed, during last part of baking to
prevent over-browning. **Yield: 14 servings**

Per Serving: Fat: 3g **Carbs:** 31g **Fiber:** 2.4g **Cal:** 144

Oatmeal Muffins

1 cup rolled oats, uncooked
¾ cup plain low-fat yogurt
¼ cup water
1 cup xylitol
1 egg
2 tablespoons extra virgin olive oil
4½ tablespoons unsweetened applesauce
1¾ cups spelt flour or whole wheat pastry flour
1 teaspoon baking powder
¼ teaspoon salt
½ teaspoon baking soda
½ teaspoon cinnamon
¼ teaspoon cloves
¼ teaspoon mace
1 teaspoon finely grated lemon zest
½ cup raisins (optional)

Combine oats, raisins, yogurt, and water in a large bowl; cover, and let stand at room temperature for 1-2 hours. Stir in xylitol, egg, oil and applesauce; mix well. Combine flour, baking powder, salt, baking soda, spices, and lemon zest; gradually stir into oat mixture. Coat muffin cups with nonstick spray. Spoon batter into muffin pan and bake at 350º for 18-20 minutes or until a toothpick inserted in center comes out clean.
Yield: 14 muffins

Per Muffin: Fat: 3.5g **Carbs:** 31.8g **Fiber:** 3.1g **Cal:** 148

Orange Pecan Tea Bread

1¾ cups plus 2 tablespoons spelt flour or whole wheat pastry flour
½ cup xylitol
½ teaspoon salt
1 teaspoon baking soda
1½ teaspoons lecithin granules
1 teaspoon freshly grated orange zest
1 teaspoon freshly grated lemon zest
⅓ cup finely chopped pecans
1 egg
2 tablespoons extra virgin olive oil
1½ tablespoons unsweetened applesauce
1 cup freshly squeezed orange juice

Combine flour, xylitol, salt, baking soda, lecithin, orange and lemon zest, and pecans. Add remaining ingredients and mix well. Pour batter into a buttered 9"x 5"x 3" loaf pan. Bake at 350° for 35-40 minutes or until toothpick inserted in center comes out clean. Cover bread with foil, if needed, during last part of baking to prevent over-browning. **Yield: 14 servings**

Per Serving: Fat: 5g **Carbs:** 22.8g **Fiber:** 2.4g **Cal:** 139

Peanut Butter Muffins

1½ cups spelt flour or whole wheat pastry flour
¼ teaspoon salt
2 teaspoons baking powder
½ cup plus 3 tablespoons xylitol
½ cup unsweetened applesauce
½ cup peanut butter
¾ cup plain low-fat yogurt
2 tablespoons water
1 teaspoon vanilla extract

Combine flour, salt, baking powder, and xylitol in a large bowl. In a medium bowl, combine applesauce, peanut butter, yogurt, water, and vanilla extract. Add peanut butter mixture to dry ingredients and stir just until flour is moistened. Coat muffin pan cups with non-stick spray. Spoon batter into muffin pan, and bake at 350° for 15-20 minutes or until toothpick inserted in center comes out clean. **Yield: 12 muffins**

Per Muffin: Fat: 6g **Carbs:** 27.3g **Fiber:** 3.7g **Cal:** 167

Peanut Butter and Chocolate Chip Muffins

Coarsely chop 2 bars (1.5 oz. each) of maltitol-sweetened dark chocolate and stir into dry ingredients before adding peanut butter mixture. See Peanut Butter Muffins recipe, page 56. **Yield: 12 muffins**

Per Muffin: **Fat:** 8.5g **Carbs:** 27.5 **Fiber:** 4.4g **Cal:** 199

Pumpkin Streusel Muffins With Cream Cheese Centers

Muffins:
- 1 egg
- ½ cup plain low-fat yogurt
- 2 tablespoons water
- ¾ cup plus 2 tablespoons canned pumpkin
- 2 tablespoons extra-virgin olive oil
- 1¾ cup spelt flour or whole wheat pastry flour
- ½ cup plus 2 tablespoons xylitol
- ¼ teaspoon salt
- ½ teaspoon nutmeg
- 2 teaspoons baking powder
- 1 teaspoon cinnamon
- 1 tablespoon lecithin granules
- 3 ounces reduced-fat cream cheese

Streusel Topping:
- ¼ cup xylitol
- ½ teaspoon cinnamon
- 1½ teaspoons unsalted butter
- 3 tablespoons finely ground almonds or pecans
- 1 tablespoon quick-cooking oats

In medium bowl, combine egg, yogurt, water, pumpkin, and oil; mix well. In another bowl, stir together flour, xylitol, salt, nutmeg, baking powder, cinnamon, and lecithin. Add dry ingredients to pumpkin mixture and stir just until flour is moistened. Coat muffin cups with non-stick spray. Spoon batter into muffin pan, and fill half full. Divide cream cheese into 12 equal pieces. Place one piece on batter in each cup, then top with remaining batter. Combine ingredients for the streusel topping. Mix well and sprinkle evenly over each muffin. Bake at 350° for 18-22 minutes or until lightly browned. Best when served warm. **Yield: 12 muffins**

Per Muffin: **Fat:** 6.6g **Carbs:** 31.6g **Fiber:** 3.4g **Cal:** 183

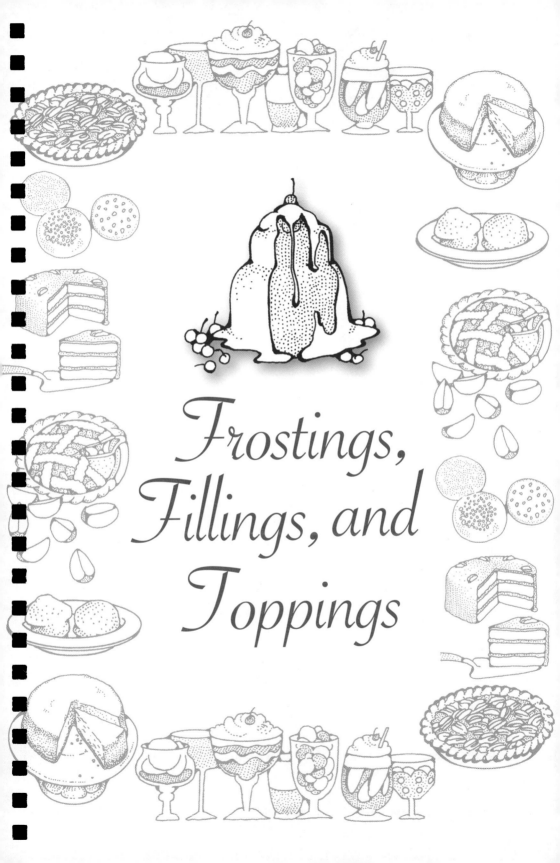

Frostings,
Fillings, and
Toppings

Cherry Topping for Black Forest Cake

10 ounce package frozen dark sweet cherries, thawed
⅓ cup powdered xylitol
¼ teaspoon cherry flavoring
2 teaspoons arrowroot powder
1 tablespoon cherry liqueur
1 tablespoon water

Strain cherries. Should yield approximately ½ cup of juice. Place juice in a small saucepan, stir in powdered xylitol, cherry flavoring, and arrowroot powder. Bring to a boil over medium low heat, stirring constantly, and cook until translucent. Remove from heat, and add cherry liqueur, water, and cherries. **Yield: 16 servings on Black Forest Cake**

Per Serving: Fat: 0.1g **Carbs:** 7.4g **Fiber:** 0.4g **Cal:** 26

Chocolate Ganache

3 ounces unsweetened chocolate bar
½ cup whipping cream
¾ cup xylitol
¾ cup reduced-fat sour cream

In double boiler set over hot water, melt the chocolate. Stir in the whipping cream, and gradually add the xylitol, stirring until it is completely dissolved. Remove from heat, and stir in sour cream until thoroughly blended. **Yield: 1½ cups**

Notes: 6 ounces of maltitol-sweetened dark chocolate bars may be used instead of the 3 ounces unsweetened chocolate: for this application, delete the xylitol in the recipe.

This version of chocolate ganache contains much less fat than the traditional recipe. Chocolate Ganache is very versatile. When warm, it may be poured over cake and serve as a glaze. As the ganache cools, it becomes more firm, and may be used as a filling between cake layers. The cooled ganache may also be whipped and used as a rich and creamy frosting.

Per Tablespoon: Fat: 4.3g **Carbs:** 8.1g **Fiber:** 0.6g **Cal:** 59

Chocolate Sauce

    3 ounces unsweetened chocolate bar
    ¾ cup water
    1½ tablespoons unsalted butter
    1 cup xylitol
    1½ teaspoons vanilla extract

In double boiler, melt chocolate in water; add butter, and stir until melted. Add xylitol and stir until it has completely dissolved. Transfer to direct heat and bring chocolate mixture to a low boil. Let boil for 3-5 minutes, stirring frequently. Remove from heat and stir in vanilla extract. **Yield: 1⅛ cups sauce**

Note: This sauce is thin when warm, but thickens as it cools in the refrigerator. Delicious when spooned over ice cream or cake.

Per Tablespoon: Fat: 3.5g **Carbs:** 12.2g **Fiber:** 0.8g **Cal:** 59

Coconut-Pecan Frosting

    5 tablespoons unsalted butter
    5 tablespoons unsweetened applesauce
    4 teaspoons lecithin granules
    ¾ cup xylitol
    4 tablespoons nonfat dry milk powder
    4 egg yolks
    ½ cup plus 2 tablespoons water
    ⅛ teaspoon maple flavoring
    1¼ teaspoons vanilla extract
    ⅔ cup coconut
    ⅔ cup chopped pecans

Combine butter, applesauce, lecithin, xylitol, milk powder, and egg yolks in a saucepan. Slowly stir in water. Cook over medium heat, stirring constantly, for 10 minutes. Strain into bowl, and stir in maple flavoring, vanilla extract, coconut, and pecans. Spread on cooled cake. **Yield: 24 servings when used on German Chocolate Cake**

Per Serving: Fat: 7.2g **Carbs:** 8g **Fiber:** 0.5g **Cal:** 89

Créme de Menthe Cream Cheese Frosting

4 tablespoons unsalted butter, softened
8 ounce package reduced-fat cream cheese, softened
4 tablespoons xylitol
1½ tablespoons green crème de menthe

Beat butter and cream cheese at high speed with an electric mixer until light and fluffy. Gradually beat in xylitol; stir in crème de menthe. Frosts one 9" x 13" cake. **Yield: 24 servings when used on Chocolate Cake Squares**

Per Serving: **Fat:** 3.5g **Carbs:** 3.1g **Fiber:** 0g **Cal:** 46

Lemon Cream Cheese Frosting

½ cup unsalted butter, softened
8 ounce package reduced-fat cream cheese, softened
½ cup plus 1 tablespoon xylitol
1 tablespoon fresh squeezed lemon juice
1 tablespoon grated lemon zest

Beat butter and cream cheese at high speed with an electric mixer until light and fluffy. Gradually beat in xylitol; stir in lemon juice and lemon zest. **Yield: 20 servings when used on Carrot Cake**

Per Serving: **Fat:** 6.4g **Carbs:** 6.3g **Fiber:** 0g **Cal:** 78

Mocha Cream Cheese Frosting

4 tablespoons unsalted butter, softened
8 ounce package reduced fat cream cheese, softened
4 tablespoons xylitol
3 tablespoons unsweetened cocoa powder
1 teaspoon vanilla extract
1 teaspoon coffee extract
½ teaspoon fresh squeezed orange or lemon juice

Beat butter and cream cheese at high speed with an electric mixer until light and fluffy. Combine xylitol and cocoa powder; gradually beat into cream cheese mixture. Stir in extracts and juice. Frosts one 9" x 13" cake. **Yield: 24 servings when used on Chocolate Cake Squares**

Per Serving: Fat: 3.6g **Carbs:** 3.1g **Fiber:** 0.1g **Cal:** 44

Seven-Minute Frosting

2 egg whites
1 cup xylitol
¼ teaspoon cream of tartar
¼ cup water
1 teaspoon vanilla extract

Combine egg whites, xylitol, cream of tartar, and water in top of double boiler. Beat at high speed for 1 minute. Bring water in pan to rapid boil; beat for another 7 minutes or until peaks form when beater is raised. Remove from heat, and transfer frosting to large bowl. Add vanilla extract, and beat until frosting reaches spreading consistency. **Yield: 2½ cups, or 12-16 servings. Generously fills and frosts 2 layers or a 9" x 13" x 2" cake**

Note: If desired, another flavoring may be substituted for the vanilla extract.

Per Serving: Fat: 0g **Carbs:** 12g **Fiber:** 0g **Cal:** 32

Vanilla Cream Custard Filling

⅓ cup xylitol
2 tablespoons arrowroot powder
¼ teaspoon salt
2 cups milk
3 egg yolks
1 teaspoon vanilla extract

Combine xylitol, arrowroot powder, and salt in medium saucepan. Gradually stir in milk, then egg yolks, until well blended. Cook over medium heat, stirring with whisk constantly, until mixture thickens and boils. Continue stirring with whisk, allow to boil 1 minute; remove from heat. Stir in vanilla extract. Pour custard into bowl, cover with wax paper, press down on paper until it touches custard. Refrigerate for 30 minutes or until custard is cool, but not set. This filling is used in Boston Cream Pie, page 21. **Yield: 2¼ cups or 12 servings**

Per Serving: **Fat:** 2.6g **Carbs:** 8.3g **Fiber:** 0g **Cal:** 58

Whipped Cream Frosting

1 teaspoon unflavored gelatin
2 tablespoons water
1 cup whipping cream
2 tablespoons powdered xylitol

Sprinkle gelatin over water in a small glass measuring cup; allow gelatin to soften for 5 minutes. Place the cup with the gelatin and water in a microwave, and briefly warm the mixture (5-10 seconds).

Have the beaters and mixing bowl chilled before preparing the frosting. Beat the whipping cream and powdered xylitol until the cream begins to thicken. While beating the cream, gradually pour the warm gelatin mixture in a steady stream onto the cream. Beat cream just until stiff peaks are formed. Do not overbeat. Keeps well in the refrigerator for up to 3 days. This frosting is used with Black Forest Cake, page 4. **Yield: 2 cups or 16 servings**

Per Serving: **Fat:** 5.5g **Carbs:** 1.9g **Fiber:** 0g **Cal:** 56

Drinks, Ice Creams, Etc.

French Vanilla Ice Cream

2 cups fat-free milk
¼ cup arrowroot powder
1 1/3 cups xylitol
4 egg yolks
2 ½ teaspoons vanilla extract
1 cup reduced-fat sour cream
1 cup whipping cream, whipped just until barely firm
2 tablespoons powdered xylitol

Place milk in a small saucepan and heat to almost boiling. Remove from heat and set aside. Combine arrowroot powder and xylitol in a medium bowl. Thoroughly beat egg yolks into xylitol mixture. Slowly add scalded milk to egg mixture, stirring until well blended. Transfer to top of double boiler, and cook over boiling water, stirring constantly, until thick and smooth. Strain, if necessary. Stir in vanilla extract, and pour mixture into a large bowl. Stir in sour cream until thoroughly combined, cover bowl, and refrigerate until well chilled.

Gradually beat powdered xylitol into whipping cream; continue beating until soft peaks form. Gently fold whipped cream into chilled custard mixture. Transfer to ice cream maker and freeze. **Yield: 1½ quarts or twelve ½ cup servings**

Per Serving: **Fat:** 10.3g **Carbs:** 30.2g **Fiber:** 0g **Cal:** 193

Rich Chocolate Ice Cream

Follow above directions for French Vanilla Ice Cream, except:

Melt 2 ounces unsweetened chocolate bar; gradually stir into custard before refrigerating. **Yield: 1½ quarts or twelve ½ cup servings**

Per Serving: **Fat:** 12.9g **Carbs:** 31.8g **Fiber:** 0.8g **Cal:** 217

Note: These recipes make just the right amount to use in a small, automatic ice cream maker.

Peach Ice Cream

1 cup xylitol
1 tablespoon arrowroot powder
1 cup whole milk
2 cups peach puree (from peaches that have been peeled, pitted, and whirled in food processor for a few seconds)
2 tablespoons freshly squeezed lemon juice
1 cup whipping cream, whipped just until barely firm (overwhipped cream will freeze in lumps)

Mix together xylitol and arrowroot powder; gradually stir in milk, and cook until thick, stirring constantly. Transfer mixture to a large bowl and refrigerate until cold. Stir in peach puree and lemon juice, and refrigerate until mixture is well chilled. Fold in whipped cream just before pouring mixture into ice cream freezer. **Yield: 1½ quarts or twelve ½ cup servings**

Per Serving: **Fat:** 8g **Carbs:** 21.4g **Fiber:** 0.5g **Cal:** 136

Strawberry Ice Cream

2 cups strawberry puree (unsweetened strawberries that have been pureed in food processor)
¾ cup xylitol, divided
1 tablespoon arrowroot powder
1 cup milk
½ teaspoon vanilla extract
1 cup whipping cream, whipped just until barely firm (overwhipped cream will freeze in lumps)

Stir strawberry puree and ¼ cup xylitol together until xylitol dissolves; refrigerate until well chilled. Combine remaining ½ cup xylitol with arrowroot powder; gradually stir in milk, and cook until thick, stirring constantly. Transfer mixture to a large bowl and refrigerate until cold. Stir strawberry puree and vanilla extract into milk mixture. Fold in whipped cream just before pouring mixture into ice cream freezer. **Yield: 1½ quarts or twelve ½ cup servings**

Per Serving: **Fat:** 8.2g **Carbs:** 17.8g **Fiber:** 1.4g **Cal:** 129

Note: These recipes make just the right amount to use in a small, automatic ice cream maker.

8 cups cold filtered water
8 regular size (or 2 family size) tea bags
1½ cups (minus 1 tablespoon) xylitol
7 cups cold filtered water

Bring 8 cups cold water to a boil. Remove from heat, add tea bags, and cover. Allow tea to steep for 5-10 minutes, and remove tea bags. Add xylitol, and stir until completely dissolved. Stir in 7 cups cold water and refrigerate. Pour into ice-filled glasses, and serve with lemon slices. Very refreshing! **Yield: approximately 1 gallon iced tea or sixteen 8 ounce servings**

Per Serving: **Fat:** 0g **Carbs:** 17.3g **Fiber:** 0g **Cal:** 43

Lemonade

1½ cups freshly squeezed lemon juice
6 cups cold filtered water
1 cup plus 2 tablespoons xylitol

Combine lemon juice and cold water. Stir in xylitol until dissolved. Pour into ice-filled glasses. **Yield: 2 quarts or eight 8 ounce servings**

Per Serving: **Fat:** 0g **Carbs:** 31.1g **Fiber:** 0g **Cal:** 79

Sweetened Condensed Milk

1 cup xylitol
1½ cups nonfat dry milk
4 tablespoons unsalted butter
¾ cup boiling water

Place xylitol, milk powder, butter, and boiling water in blender; process for several minutes or until mixture is smooth. Store in refrigerator until ready to use. **Yield: 1¾ cups**

Per Tablespoon: **Fat:** 1.6g **Carbs:** 8.8g **Fiber:** 0g **Cal:** 44

Prune Puree

½ cup pitted prunes
1 cup filtered water

In blender, combine prunes and water. Process on high for several minutes, or until mixture is smooth. Store in a tightly covered container in the refrigerator (stays fresh for several weeks). **Yield: 1½ cups**

Per Tablespoon: Fat: 0g **Carbs:** 2.1g **Fiber:** 0.2g **Cal:** 8

Special Ingredients

This section is devoted to providing information and guidance concerning some of the ingredients used in the recipes in this book that may be unfamiliar to you. In compiling these recipes, I have focused on using primarily whole foods, however, I chose to use liqueurs to enhance the flavor of some of the recipes.

APPLESAUCE (UNSWEETENED). This is applesauce made entirely from apples and water. Apples are naturally sweet so an added sweetener is really unnecessary. This is an excellent substitute for some of the fat in these recipes.

ARROWROOT POWDER. Arrowroot powder is a white, unrefined starch that is made from the root of a tropical American plant. It looks like cornstarch, is a natural thickening agent, and can be substituted for cornstarch on a 1 for 1 basis in pie fillings, sauces, and even ice creams. When substituting arrowroot for flour, only use half the amount of arrowroot. Arrowroot is inexpensive, and is available in health food stores.

CHOCOLATE BARS (SUGARLESS). Chocolate bars sweetened with maltitol are available in various sizes and flavors. Do not confuse sugarless bars with the unsweetened baking chocolate bars below. See Product Directory for sources.

CHOCOLATE FOR BAKING (UNSWEETENED). This form of chocolate comes in bar form, and is made of pure chocolate. It works well in some recipes, and its major advantage is that xylitol can be added to increase the sweetness of the chocolate to a semi-sweet taste.

CHERRY FLAVORING. This is an essential ingredient to enhance the cherry flavor in some recipes. Normally, I prefer to use extracts, but in this case the cherry flavoring is preferred. See Product Directory for source.

CHERRY LIQUEUR. This is a fruit liqueur produced from a distilling process using cherries. It is used to enhance the flavor of many cherry-based desserts.

COCONUT (UNSWEETENED, SHREDDED). Unsweetened and shredded or flaked coconut is available in health food stores. Fresh shredded coconut can be stored in a refrigerator for up to one week, or in a freezer for up to one year. Flaked coconut can be shredded in a food processor if the shredded product is not available.

CRÈME DE CACAO. This is a clear, chocolate-flavored liqueur produced from cocoa beans. It is a very popular liqueur and is often paired with crème de menthe in recipes.

CRÈME DE MENTHE. This is a very popular peppermint-flavored liqueur available colorless or in a green color. It is often paired with crème de cacao in recipes.

CREAM OF TARTAR. This is a substance that can be added to egg whites while beating them to form meringue. Cream of tartar increases the meringue's volume, stabilizes it, and prevents it from becoming too dry.

EXTRACTS. These are available in a large variety of flavors, depending on the flavoring ingredient they are made from. For example, vanilla extract is made from the vanilla bean. Use pure extracts, rather than flavorings, whenever possible. Exceptions are cherry flavoring and maple flavoring. See the Product Directory for sources.

EXTRA-VIRGIN OR VIRGIN OLIVE OIL. Olive oil's use over the centuries has proven it to be a stable, health-enhancing oil. Even though it is a poor source of essential fatty acids, it contains a high percentage of monounsaturated fatty acids that lower only the LDL or "bad cholesterol". If the olive oil is not labeled 'unrefined', the oil has undergone numerous refining processes, has been essentially stripped of any nutritional value, and has undergone molecular changes that can adversely affect our health. All virgin olive oils are unrefined, therefore, only virgin or extra-virgin olive oils are recommended. Extra-virgin olive oils are of the finest quality and must meet strict guidelines. When extra virgin olive oil is used in small quantities, the flavor of the basic recipe is not affected, and the taste of the olive oil is not detectable.

FRUIT SPREAD. The fruit spreads that are recommended for use in these recipes are sweetened only with fruit juices and contain no added sugar. Fruit spreads that are sweetened with maltitol are also available. See Product Directory for sources.

GELATIN (UNFLAVORED). Gelatin is an animal by-product and is available in grocery stores. Kosher gelatin, which contains no animal products and may be preferred by vegetarians and vegans, is made from vegetable gum, tapioca dextrin, and acids. Powdered gelatin comes packaged four or more to a box. Each package contains 2 ¼ teaspoons of gelatin and will gel two cups of liquid. To soften gelatin, sprinkle it over a cold liquid and let stand for 2 to 3 minutes, then either warm the liquid, stirring until the gelatin is dissolved, or add a hot liquid to the gelatin mixture and stir until the gelatin is dissolved. Gelatin becomes firm when chilled in the refrigerator. See Product Directory for source of Kosher gelatin.

KAHLUA. Kahlua is a coffee-flavored liqueur.

LECITHIN GRANULES. Lecithin is a by-product of refined soybean oil. It is nutritious and helps to create a softer texture in breads and cakes. The granules contain only about half the fat of butter. It is available in liquid and granular form; however, the granules are much easier to work with. Be sure to use unflavored granules so that the flavor of the recipe is not affected. Lecithin may be purchased at health food stores.

NON-FAT DRY MILK POWDER. This is whole milk that has had the fat and water removed, which means that the fat-soluble vitamins are also missing. However, this form of milk is excellent for use in recipes for whipped toppings and sweetened condensed milk so that xylitol can be used as the only sweetener.

PEANUT BUTTER. Be sure to select pure peanut butter made from roasted peanuts only with no sweetener added. Sometimes a small amount of salt is added to the peanut butter for flavor.

POWDERED XYLITOL. This is granulated xylitol that has been ground to a fine powder. It can be substituted for powdered sugar on a one-for-one basis. Xylitol can be ground to a powder in a blender, but the process is time-consuming. It is available commercially.

PRUNE PUREE. This is made by placing prunes and water in a blender and pureeing until the mixture is smooth. It is an excellent substitute for some of the fat in recipes.

SPELT FLOUR. Spelt is a type of "hard" wheat used since ancient times. Even though spelt contains gluten, many individuals with wheat allergies have found this grain to be more digestible and to cause fewer allergy problems than other gluten-containing grains. Spelt flour is available in health food stores.

TOFU. This is a soft, relatively tasteless food made from processed soybean curd. It may be purchased from health food stores and grocery stores.

TRIPLE SEC. This is an orange-flavored liqueur made from orange skins. It is less expensive and has less alcohol content than the two other orange-flavored liqueurs, Curacao and Grand Marnier, which may be substituted if desired.

UNSALTED BUTTER. Unsalted butter is much purer than salted butter and has a better flavor, in my opinion. Salt is usually added to butter to help preserve it and to mask any off-flavors and poor quality. I recommend that you use only U.S. Grade AA sweet cream unsalted butter.

WHOLE WHEAT PASTRY FLOUR. This is flour made from "soft" wheat that is more finely ground than regular whole-wheat flour. It may be used to replace all-purpose flour on a cup-for-cup basis.

YOGURT (LOW-FAT). Yogurt is made from milk that has had cultures added in order to make it curdle. It has the consistency of custard, and is a rich source of acidophilus and other beneficial bacteria. Plain yogurt is an excellent substitute for some of the fat in baked goods recipes. Most flavored yogurt sold commercially contains refined sugar, artificial colors and flavors, very little fruit, and many other ingredients to enhance its look and taste but add little or no nutritional value. If you want a more nutritious treat, my recommendation is to purchase unflavored low-fat yogurt and add fruit and xylitol.

ZEST (GRATED LEMON OR ORANGE RIND). You should grate only the colored part of the rind from these fruits, not the white portion under the rind as this has a bitter taste. Zest adds color and flavor to recipes. Always wash fruits thoroughly and dry them well prior to grating.

Choosing Cookware and Bakeware

I strongly recommend against using aluminum cookware and baking ware for several reasons. Aluminum pots and baking pans should not be used because most cooking utensils can easily scratch the inside surfaces which can cause some of the aluminum to be leached into the foods being cooked. The body then absorbs this leached aluminum when the food is eaten, and eventually it migrates into the cells of the brain and nervous system. It is suspected that an accumulation of excess aluminum in these organs is related to Alzheimer's disease, which is now one of the five leading causes of death in the United States. Also, when foods are cooked or stored in aluminum cookware, a substance that neutralizes the digestive juices can be produced, which may result in the development of acidosis and ulcers. However, aluminum bakeware can be used if the interior surfaces are coated with butter and then lined with wax or parchment paper, which should be buttered and floured prior to adding the ingredients for baking.

Other cookware to be avoided includes all pots and pans with such non-stick coatings as Teflon and other types of synthetic materials. These coatings, as a general rule, do not hold up well, and when scratched, they can flake off and react with the food being cooked in them. Ultimately, the chemicals in these coatings end up in the body. Bakeware with non-stick coatings may be used; however, great care should be used in removing food baked in these pans. This type of bakeware is easily scratched, so use a plastic utensil to remove food from it instead of using a metal utensil or any other sharp object. If this bakeware becomes scratched, it may still be used if it is treated in the same manner as described above for aluminum bakeware.

Glass, stainless steel or cast iron are excellent choices for cookware and baking pans. I prefer to use Pyrex glass pie plates because the glass distributes the heat evenly and it is easy to determine visually when the crust is done. Stainless steel saucepans are excellent choices because they are very durable and easy to clean when the following suggestions are considered: (1) When cooking with gas, made sure that the flame touches only the bottom of the saucepan, and does not touch the sides of the pan; (2) Cool pots and pans prior to rinsing and soaking; (3) Don't allow an empty pan to sit on a hot burner, don't allow foods in the cookware to become so dry that they burn, and don't let liquids boil off completely;

(4) Stainless steel is not a very good conductor of heat itself, so in choosing stainless steel cookware, select those brands that are made of a heavy gauge and have copper or laminated aluminum bottoms as this will help to evenly distribute the heat and prevent burning over high heat; (5) Use wood or one of the new plastic material utensils to avoid scarring or scratching the highly-polished interiors to make the cookware easier to keep clean.

Cast iron cookware is very versatile – it can be used in the oven or for range-top cooking – and if cared for properly, it will last practically forever. After it has been heated, it evenly distributes the heat and also retains it quite well. The secret to using cast iron cookware is to keep it seasoned to prevent rusting and to make it non-sticking. To season cast iron, spread salad oil on the inside, place in a 250° oven for several hours, and reapply the oil as it is absorbed. Remove the cookware from the oven and allow it to cool completely. Wipe off the excess oil with paper towels, and the cookware is now ready to use. Seasoned cast-iron cookware needs very little washing – just rinse under very hot water and wipe dry. Food comes out of cast-iron cookware very easily; however, as the seasoning wears off over time, food may begin to stick to it. To remove the stuck food, scrub the cookware with a plastic abrasive pad, and again follow the above directions to renew the seasoning. As an added protection against rusting, dry cast-iron cookware over medium-low heat for a few minutes after washing.

Product Directory

Chocolate Bars (Maltitol Sweetened):

Cavalier Belgian Chocolate Bars and Pure De-lite Chocolate Bars are available from:
The Low Carb Connoisseur
1520 East Greenville Street
Anderson, SC 29621
(888) 339-2477
www.lowcarb.com

LaNouba Belgian chocolate bars are available from:
Global Sweet Polyols
125 Tremont Street
Rehoboth, MA 02769
(800) 601-0688
www.globalsweet.com

Pure De-lite Belgian Chocolate Bars are available from:
Pure De-Lite Products, Inc.
P.O. Box 50885
Provo, UT 84605-0885
(866) 456-2272
www.puredeliteproducts.com

Ross Chocolates are Belgian chocolate bars and are available from:
Platinum Distribution, Inc.
A Ross Chocolates Distribution Company
Wilmington, DE 19808
(877) 277-2892
www.rossdirect.com

Organic Dry Milk Powder:
Organic whole milk powder and non-fat dry milk powder
Humboldt Creamery Association
572 Hwy 1
Fortuna, CA 95540-9711
(707) 725-6182
www.humboldtcreamery.com

Organic buttermilk blend and organic non-fat dry milk powder:
Organic Valley Family of Farms
CROPP Cooperative
507 West Main Street
La Farge, WI 54639
(888) 444-6455
www.organicvalley.com

Extracts:
Flavorganics sells vanilla extract and other organic pure flavored extracts through various distributors to health food stores. Tree of Life is a distributor of Flavorganics.
Flavorganics
268 Doremus Avenue
Newark, NJ 07105
(973) 344-8014
www.flavorganics.com

Flavorings:

Cherry and Maple Flavoring, available from Spicery Shoppe – they sell directly to health food stores; Tree of Life also distributes this brand. These products are also available over the Internet at:

www.somethingbetter
naturalfoods.com

Fruit Jams sweetened with maltitol:

LaNouba Imported Sugar-Free Jams, available from:

Global Sweet Polyols
125 Tremont Street
Rehoboth, MA 02769
(800) 601-0688
www.globalsweet.com

Fruit Spreads sweetened with fruit juices:

Harvest Moon Fruit Spread, distributed by Tree of Life, Inc. to health food stores and grocery stores:

Tree of Life, Inc.
P.O. Box 9000
St. Augustine, FL 32085-9000
(800) 260-2424
www.treeoflife.com

Village Organics Fruit Spread, available from:

Village Organics, Inc.
18637-E Northline Drive
Cornelius, NC 28031
(800) 713-3198
www.villageorganics.com

Kosher Gelatin:

Vip Foods, Inc.
1080 Wyckoff Avenue
Ridgewood, NY 11385
(718) 821-5330 or
(800) 835-6535
www.vipfoodsinc.com

Index

About the Author

Karen Edwards has had a lifelong interest in cooking and became acquainted with natural methods of food preparation and the necessity for better nutrition through the La Leche League after the birth of her son. After developing several chronic health problems, she began to investigate non-traditional healing modalities. In order to gain a more thorough knowledge of natural healing and lifestyle modification, she enrolled in a doctoral program at Clayton College of Natural Health. Because of her intense interest in natural healing, she overcame the chronic health problems that had been affecting her. Upon completion and acceptance of her doctoral dissertation, "Reversing Periodontal Disease," she received her PhD in Holistic Nutrition from Clayton College of Natural Health. She has served as a volunteer in a cooperative health food store, operated her own nutritional supplement store, and presented talks to various groups about healthy cooking methods and lifestyle changes. She currently resides with her husband and son in Gulf Breeze, Florida.